START UP GANG

Stories between
dream & success

by Andy Nathan

This is for my grandfather, Mel Gurewitz.
Your radiant smile will be missed, and you leave a gap at the family dinner table with your absence. Thank you for all the great memories!

➡Join our Free Mastermind Webinar!
Learn how to get your idea out there, and start your ideal business.

Starting a business ranks up there with buying a home and getting your license. This is a defining moment, when you have the opportunity to follow your dreams. The challenge is that generally we procrastinate, before we make that first step towards being an entrepreneur.

Instead we must learn how to just get it out there for the world to see. More perfect business ideas have never been launched than average products that changed the world. Which you would prefer to launch?

If you are ready to just get it out there, then I am inviting you to a free two session mastermind training we will be holding in September to help you get started.

This mastermind teaches you how to defeat your fears, and take those first brave steps to a better, freer future. The perfect business that never gets launched is not perfect!

http://startupgap.com/mastermind

Thanks,

Andy Nathan

P.S. Space is limited to the first 100 registered attendees, and these LIVE trainings always fill up fast. Claim your spot now at *http://startupgap.com/mastermind!*

➡Index

This is the book I always wanted to read. That crazy book that actually discusses what happens to entrepreneurs when they go from dreams to success.

In many senses, the *Start Up Gap* is a battle between perfection and getting it out there. When is good, good enough? When do you have to spend more time perfecting your craft?

By mastering that combination of perfection and getting it out there, you will master the *Start Up Gap*. This book will not only provide you with the stories of how others achieved that balance, but step by step instructions for you to do this as well.

WHAT IS THE *START UP GAP*?

The *Start Up Gap* is about:
- Overcoming your biggest fear
- Taking action
- Working hard when no one notices
- Getting it out there when it is not perfect!

The stories on these pages can help us understand these concepts. To repeat mistakes needlessly, and not follow solid principles of success is a true travesty that I hope this book will help you avoid.

So, how do most entrepreneurs go from dreams to success? Until now, almost no resources provided an answer.

Take this segment from Bill Gates profile on *Wikipedia*.

"Microsoft became independent of MITS in late 1976, and it continued to develop programming language software for various systems.[39] The company moved from Albuquerque to its new home in Bellevue, Washington on January 1, 1979.

IBM approached Microsoft in July 1980 regarding its upcoming personal computer, the IBM PC."

What is missing in this paragraph?

Personally, I read this and think; they got lucky with a contract with IBM. However, a deeper look, tells us that in fact it was 4 years of hard work that made the deal possible.

How did they pay the bills in the meantime? Did they face any challenges? Where did they make their money in the early years? Did competitors treat them seriously? What made Microsoft so special in 1980 that IBM approached them?

I want to know about Microsoft's *Start Up Gap*! I want to know about the *Start Up Gap* of all companies. The truth about how a company succeeds is not in the successes you hear about on the news. Instead, entrepreneurs toil for years without recognition or a guarantee of success. How did they deal with rejection? How did they channel rejection into an action plan?

Throughout history, we have accepted the notion that great people succeed because of their skills, ideas, and persistence. However, we shy away from knowing the details of what they had to do to persist.

Entrepreneurs do not always listen to successful people's stories. We do not learn from their mistakes.

That is not acceptable! Before now we had a novel with no beginning. I wanted to change this. With the help of this book we will understand these companies' origin stories.

UNDERSTANDING THE GAP

Before we get to the stories, let's clarify a few things.

First, the vast majority of information in this book comes from two sources: my blog posts on historical leaders (A.K.A people who passed away and cannot be interviewed) and current entrepreneurs (people I can interview.)

The main source comes from the research done during building the *Start Up Gap* blog and through the interviews conducted through Google Hangouts over the course of the past 9 months.

The YouTube videos of the interviews are available at:

http://goo.gl/4kMmcR

The transcripts and research posts are available at:

http://startupgap.com/blog

Second, for the sake of my sanity, and not to bore you with long titles throughout this book, when I refer to business professionals, entrepreneurs, and leaders I am referring to the people we interviewed. For simplicity and accuracy, we will call them the *Start Up Gappers* or *Gappers.*

Third, what we discuss here are the principles of success. These are the principles that our speakers found useful on their way to success. There are many visions of success, please keep in mind that it can mean different things to different people.

As **Carmen Mandich** stated, "Success is not measured by how much money you have, how many places you have been, how many friends you have or how high you are in the company. It is the whole feeling you sense when you are surrounded by those you have helped and make you feel whole. It is the people that contributed to your well-being."

What I hope you will get from this book are the seven principles you can use to get to your place of well-being faster and without all the challenges people in this book faced.

➡1: Breaking Down the Start Up Gap

Part of what I wanted to do when I came up with the concept for Start Up Gap was to determine, roughly, how long it takes to become successful.

For those who are a bit numbers averse, my deepest apologies. This chapter explains why the *Start Up Gap* works, so you will understand the principles we discuss in the rest of the book.

NUMBERS CAVEATS

1. DATES ARE A ... YEAH!

First, I did my best to analyze when Gappers started and became successful. However, this is as much art as it is science. What I discovered was that most successful people started off in another field first, and later made the switch to their chosen business. In this book I decided to focus solely on when a person started the endeavor that got them to success.

2. NOW I AM SUCCESSFUL ... WAIT ... NOW I AM ...

Second, what I find interesting is how many Gappers do not consider themselves successful.

Dino Dogan, Triberr co-founder, put it best. "Frankly, I am afraid to feel successful, because when you feel success you feel contented. When you feel contented, you tend to get lazy, and when you get lazy, you get stupid."

START UP GAP BREAKDOWN

To obtain better statistics on this topic, I went outside the in-depth case studies I use throughout the rest of this book. In order to get the best information, we looked into lists of the top leaders, entertainers, and business professionals alive today.

While figuring out dates is not an exact science, I did my best to use benchmark dates when someone started on a venture or in an industry, as well as the dates when they succeeded in a particular project or business.

Here are a few ground rules that I used to determine the *Start Up Gap* for the entrepreneurs included in this list.

1. You must not inherit the company (J.P. Morgan), or receive a large inheritance of money to start up the company (Frederick W. Smith).
1. The start (dream) date usually coincides with the start in an industry (Michael Steltzner) or with the founding of the company (Dwan Twyford).
1. The success is either provided by the Gapper during the interview (Liz Strauss, Chef Dennis), or correlates to a financial success (Mark Cuban, George Lucas)

(START UP GAP TIME TABLE)

START UP GAP (ALL NUMBERS ARE IN YEARS)	START UP GAP AVERAGE	MEDIAN START UP GAP	FASTEST 25% START UP GAP	SLOWEST 25% START UP GAP
INTERNET/TECH	6.34	4	2.57	13.14
BUSINESS	10.52	8.5	2.63	22.5
LEADERS	14.67	12.5	7.33	33
ENTERTAINMENT	10	9	4.25	17
ALIVE	4.76	7	2.72	16.38
DECEASED	15.1	10.5	7.8	27.6
All	6.68	8	2.72	10.72

(Sample size: 91 business owners, leaders, and entertainers. Get a free copy of the Start Up Gap list of entrepreneurs: http://startupgap.com/list)

Clarification on the breakdown of industries listed above.
- Internet/Tech — marketers, digital agencies, app developers, social networkers, bloggers, etc.
- Business — A general umbrella for every other type of business owner.
- Leaders — Political, Religious, & Moral Leaders
- Entertainers — Actors, Media, Art, and Music

START UP GAP HIGHLIGHTS

Here are three highlights that we found extremely interesting that we want to explore in further detail.

AVERAGE TIME TO SUCCEED

The average time for dreams to success is 6.68 years, with current Gappers succeeding in 4.76 years.

While many achieved success earlier than this, some Gappers spent almost 30 years to get to the level of success we know them for today. Ray Kroc took 36 years, Andrew Carnegie took 33 years, and Abraham Lincoln took 27 years.

What I found even more interesting is that 2 years seems to be the minimum time across all subsets of successful people to make something happen. Only three people (Gerald Oginski, Jeff Bullas, Jeff Bezos) succeeded in their first year. Not surprisingly, all three had previous life experiences.

ALIVE VERSUS DECEASED

You hear the idea that success is easier today than at any time in history. We decided to test out that theory.

We removed any deceased historical leader or entrepreneur from the Gapper group. While not a statistically significant part of the test sample, the results still speak volumes.

On average, success takes 4.76 years if you are alive today.

In the past it took approximately 15.1 years on average to succeed. Even more shocking when you consider the fastest 25% of deceased *Start Up Gap*pers are still a year above the 6.68 year total average.

While there are many answers that could explain this increased success ratio, it is largely due to the fact that we have so many resources available to help us achieve our dream these days.

INTERNET/TECH

While owning a business online is just like owning any other type of business, there is a key difference.

People have this absurd notion that success online takes only two minutes to happen. If not, then it does not happen at all.

What we found was that the average start time of the digital marketers was 6.34 years. The bottom 25% took 13.14 years. While this is the lowest among all subsets, 10 years is still a very long time.

START UP GAP SIMILARITIES

Even more interesting than the startup times were the Gappers' experiences on their road from dreams to success.

CHALLENGES

First, many of the entrepreneurs we talked to encountered similar challenges. These included people mocking their dreams, not having the right technical/organizational abilities, lack of funds, and fear issues. Most of the challenges fell into these four categories.

CHALLENGES

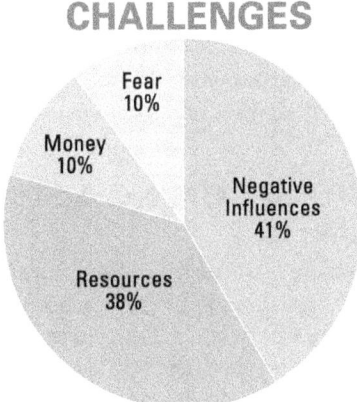

Based on the chart above, 41% of Gappers had a negative influence that they had to overcome. Amazing how sometimes those closest to us provide the most resistance to your dreams.

The truth is new things scare people. You are scary, because they see you doing something amazing. Do not worry about that. Focus instead on how you will help people.

HABITS

Looking at the habits of the Gappers other trends emerge.

HABITS

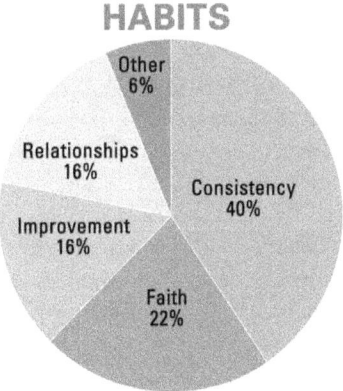

As Og Mandino states in The Greatest Salesman in the World, "In truth, the only difference between those who have failed and those who succeeded lies in the difference of their habits. Good habits are the key to all success. Bad habits are the unlocked door to failure."

What are the habits of the Gappers? An overwhelming, 40% of them stated that consistency and hard work are their greatest habit. In fact, common words that were heard throughout all my interviews were, "focus, consistency, and doing what I need to do."

Consistency plays a large part in the road to success, as we will discuss in Chapter 7. So, why did we decide to analyze the Gappers based on the start up times?

By doing so we were able to condense what the Gappers accomplished into a 7 step process for you to follow that we will discuss in the next few chapters.

SEVEN STEPS TO BECOMING A SUCCESSFUL ENTREPRENEUR

As young, eager entrepreneurs, we rush headlong into ventures, neither seeing the thorns in the bush nor the explosive power of the actions we take.

With experience, we know what works and what does not. The difference: Preparation.

My first business, my first few businesses in fact, were monumental disasters, because I neither had the knowledge nor the understanding of what it takes to do it right. If I had, I might have hid in a hole for the rest of my life.

Now that I have been down in the trenches long enough, I acquired the entrepreneurial spirit, passion, and consistency.

To develop this spirit, you need to clarify what you want in your business, then The Seven Steps of the *Start Up Gap* will help you determine the best ways to use that spirit.

It is not enough to examine what the Gappers did to succeed; we must improve upon their process.

THE SEVEN *START UP GAP* STEPS:

1. **Month of action** — The biggest challenge for new entrepreneurs is focus. We created an exercise to help entrepreneurs get it done as they start on their journey.
2. **Prepare for moments of crisis** — Challenges happen in business. Learn how to face them with confidence.
3. **Sharpen your principles** — Now that we have worked with getting you out there to face your fears, and to take action you need to develop a set of guiding principles.
4. **Find a team of believers** — "I am a self-made man, the proud business owner with 1000 employees tells you." Do you ever hear similar statements to this? People explaining how they are self-made. No one does it all by themselves.
5. **Motivate yourself every day** — Motivation is an everyday thing. Hour by hour, day by day, your emotions and actions determine where you go.
6. **Get into the habit of success** — Success is not a magical formula. It is a habit. Every Gapper did something day in and day out before creating something truly memorable. Even young heroes like Alexander the Great and Einstein spent years on their craft.
7. **Become the Story of Success** — As a history teacher, I recognize that life is all about the story. Learn the principles, and you have a blueprint. Understand the story, and you have a mentor.

➡2. Start the Dream

When I was younger I had a crazy theory that all these successful people did so right away. Therefore, I must be a freak of nature, failing constantly.

However, the more I dug into the concept of the *Start Up Gap*, the more I discovered that I am not alone.

In fact, out of the Gappers we interviewed, only two of them made it in 1 year. Even then, they were not fresh faced college students. They were adults with family, kids, jobs, careers, etc. In the case of attorney Gerald Oginski, it was simply a new business model in the same field.

With so few of the Gappers staying put in one career, this made me realize that we need a way to help entrepreneurs avoid the potential pitfalls that can happen on the path between dreams and success.

Because of the fact that over 41% of entrepreneurs we interviewed faced a shooting squad of sorts from family, friends, and associates, we also have to compound that with the fact that so few of them want to share their idea.

Amy Baxter from Buzzy discussed this in my interview with her.

She stated, "Entrepreneurs are in love with their own brilliance and their own ideas. That makes them reluctant to share that with anyone, because they think the guy behind Willy Wonka and the Chocolate factory is hiding behind every post waiting to hear your brilliant idea, and steal it, so they make $1 million dollars."

Carol Tice said something similar when she spoke about how she built her community on her own.

"I did not ask anyone for a lot of advice when I started my community for fear that people would say that was a crazy idea … Sarah Blakely, who started Spanx, which is a Billion dollar brand.

She did not tell anyone for the first year that she was developing the product, because she thought people would laugh. 'Oh its Footless Panty hose, how are you going to create a business around that?"

The inventor of the modern razor, King Gillette, faced relentless teasing from his friends. "The razor was looked upon as a joke by all my friends, a common greeting was, 'Well, Gillette, how's the razor?' If I had been technically trained, I would have quit."

What we discover is that most entrepreneurs' dream of success only after a life in a completely different field. Without the right support, no entrepreneur has a real shot. The right support system will help. However, people support things they know you are passionate about, which means you have to know your dream, before others follow it.

WHEN IS A DREAM REAL?

This makes us wonder when a dream is real. Is it when it comes into your mind? More likely, it is when you turn that dream into reality. That requires action.

The first baby steps are monumental in transforming Gappers lives.

Dan Antonelli's interest in graphic design started when he was 13 year old reading the Hot Rod magazine. The lettering really stuck out to him. His brother asked him to create some signs, and he got interested in becoming a sign painter. It all started with a magazine, and a small task from his brother.

Fast forward a few years, he was working at a healthcare company as a graphic designer.

Dan decided to start his own business in 1995 as a way to follow his passion. He was working a full-time job, and building his business at the same time.

When he was working there he would read Sign Craft Magazine, and he felt that being in this magazine was the pinnacle of success. At the time, he was working 100 hours per week between his job and new company.

Around the end of 1996, he decided to give his business his full attention, since by then he was almost making as much on the side as he was working full-time. Moreover, his wife was a teacher, so they could rely upon her income as he built the business.

"What was really cool was that by the time I quit I had developed a decent portfolio, and I had sent my portfolio to Signcraft. The month before I quit I got a 5 page spread on Sign Craft."

Without his initial work in the field, Dan's dream would never become real. Like walking, becoming a successful entrepreneur is about putting one foot in front of the other.

EXERCISE: THE MONTH OF ACTION

My good friend, Sotiris Bassakaropoulos once told me that, "No dream can live on its own. You must constantly feed the dream. That requires action."

However, action by itself is useless. Therefore, we need to practice using action in a refined way. In Chapter 4, we will define more of what we want from these actions.

For this chapter, we must be alert and pay attention to what we want from our actions. These experiments save you time, so you do not have to jump around professions finding your calling.

Remember that only **seven** out of the *Start Up Gap*pers we discuss succeeded in their original profession. This is an indication that even the Gappers waffled at some point or another in their chosen profession. Surprise! Successful people are human.

Even scarier is the fact that 41% of them mentioned that consistency is the biggest key to success. How can you be consistent at something you do not truly like?

While focus is crucial to long-term success, nothing kills motivation like building a business in the wrong industry.

Henceforth, we created a "waffle killer" exercise to make sure you follow the **right** dream.

As someone who has experienced setting up businesses in something they have no interest in, I can tell you that building a successful business you care nothing about in the long-term is not the true road to glory and fame.

Better to play around with different ideas, until you find the one that is best for you. While this testing phase should not last too long, it is important for you to explore a few different businesses to get a feel for which one calls to you the most.

This is the reason the first chapter is about how to **start the dream.** To do this, spend a month figuring out your passion.

This is crucial for you to understand the best ways to accomplish a task. While we will discuss habits later on in this book, we need to discuss creativity first. While seemingly at odds with each, the right idea will blend creativity and habit together in one unique business model perfect for your needs.

For example, when I was in network marketing *(a grand 2 week adventure)*, I discovered that I hated most aspects of the business.

However, I admired the structure of network marketing, and looked to use it as a model to pay sales people for my real estate and social media businesses. For that reason, I will be forever grateful to the power of network marketing.

MONTH OF ACTION

You need to have a month of action. A month dedicated to testing out a new business every day. I know it sounds crazy, but what if you could market whatever business you want every day of the week without caring if it succeeds.

In essence, I am giving you permission for one month to jump in head first into businesses. A free zone to discover your passions.

That is why we need to get you into get it done thinking during the dream stage. Even for this month of action, we are still training you to plan your dreams. That is real *Start Up Gap* thinking. (Insert pat on back)

Even more important, this exercise will demonize the "what if's" of your life. What if you started your dream business? How would you know you found it? Would you still keep on looking?

Now you can decide what you want to do, without years of experience to increase your fears and destroy your motivation. Most people spend their lives talking about how they want to follow their dreams. You now have permission to start.

FIRST STEP: WHAT DO YOU WANT TO DO?

Fill out a mini calendar of events, to determine what type of business you want to test out each day. Everyone has a different amount of time available to him or her each day to work on their business. That is ok! Whatever you would normally allot to your business, allot to this exercise.

Instead of writing out your dreams, **write out 1 business you can take 2 actions on every day for the next 30 days.**

	MONDAY	TUESDAY	WEDNESDAY	THURSDAY	FRIDAY
WEEK 1	Plan/ Research your week	Create a product	Become an affiliate	Write a blog post	Create a video for YouTube
WEEK 2	Plan/ Research your week	Internet Marketer	Sell services	Sell on Ebay	Sell on Etsy
WEEK 3	Plan/ Research your week	Network Mrktng	Web developer	Financial Planner	Real Estate Investor
WEEK 4	Plan/ Research your week	Personal assistant	Author	Coach	Evaluate options

SECOND STEP: RESEARCH YOUR NEXT STEP?

Since this is to be an exercise in taking action, do not just go around doing things. Have a purpose doing them. Research what you need to get started with each business. Spend an hour each day, exploring the business you are interested in pursuing.

THIRD STEP: CONTACT THE NECESSARY PEOPLE TO GET IT DONE.

However, at a certain point jumping from place to place becomes counter-intuitive. A month is long enough to figure out your future, and short enough to push you out of your comfort zone.

This means you play around with a few ideas when you get started, and have a good story to tell later on about the best marketing strategy for your business.

RESOURCES

While you are getting it out there, consider the resources you will need to succeed. Cool! I made it rhyme, just in time!

This serves two purposes: First, you will have a platform to discuss your new ventures; & second, when you are ready to decide upon a business you will not need to start marketing from scratch.

1. **A Website.** Use WordPress, so you can update your site for your business's needs.
2. **Social Media Profiles.** Set up a profile on Facebook, Twitter, LinkedIn, and Google+.
3. **Talk to an attorney.** If you are going to incorporate, might as well use this time to get the paperwork ready. I am not an attorney, so please talk to one.
4. **Purchase Business Cards.** Vista Print gives you 100 free cards. Use those cards to start networking.
5. **Get Business Insurance Quotes.** Protect your business.

DREAM QUESTIONS:

1. What is stopping you from following your dreams?
2. What do you want?
3. What are your strengths?
4. What are your weaknesses?
5. Have you written down your dreams, so they can be goals?

➡3. Challenge Accepted

To any great dream, a great challenge will arise to thwart that dream early on. You will face detractors and situations that will challenge your ability to win in your chosen profession.

Before we go to step three, which is defining your purpose, you need to be ready for any challenge.

These challenges will define your story as you grow your business. It is the story you will tell your grandchildren about how you did ABC to build your business into XYZ.

Challenges come in all different sizes and shapes. You might even find your family and friends are your biggest detractors.

Consider David Meerman Scott, an author and speaker.

"By far my biggest challenge was convincing my colleagues that my ideas made sense. Most of them wanted to go with direct mail, cold calling, or other forms of generating attention.

I said, 'we need to create great content online, putting it out there so people find it, and then they will do business with us.'

I was a very early adopter. In the early days, it was just me talking about content marketing. Now, there are thousands of people talking about it."

Even worse, sometimes your family will become your greatest cynics. Gerald Oginski' family did not understand why he was playing around with YouTube in 2005.

"I would look at my wife, because she was my biggest detractor. Totally UN-supportive of what I was doing. She said this is never going to work, and my kid said the same thing. You are wasting your time.

No one is ever going to watch an attorney on YouTube."

They came around as he built a dedicated following on the video sharing site.

EXERCISE: PREPARE FOR ANY CHALLENGE

When someone challenges your established view of the world, it can be scary. How do you react? More important, how do you continue to build your business in an ethical manner despite the challenge.

Do something scary every day. In fact, do it first thing in the morning if possible. Getting rid of that fear allows you to accomplish more in your business. Overcoming the gap between dreams and success is an exercise in overcoming your fears.

One of the greatest insights I ever heard was, *what scares you most, is probably the biggest thing you need to do.*

When you can start tackling your fears, then you can define your purpose and mission in business.

Start the habit now, and get an edge over the large number of unfocused entrepreneurs.

CHALLENGE QUESTIONS
1. What scares you most about starting a new business?
2. How do you conquer your fears?
3. How does conquering your fears build your business?
4. Why do you have these challenges in your life?
5. How can you remove/mitigate them?

➡4. Define Your Principles

E very entrepreneur at some point in their career comes to a point where they must define who they are, and why they are in business for themselves. A moment of clarity if you will that changes how you view your business.

Nowhere was this as clear, as it was with Yaro Starak. His three principles for his ideal business took time to develop, but are things I feel most entrepreneurs understand.

"I was seeing all these people doing things online, and I have to come up with something bigger. I had this sort of holy trinity. It is not religious, but it is very important to me not just for my business, but also for my life.

#1 TIME FREEDOM — We are talking way before 4 Hour Work Week by Timothy Ferris. I was striving for something like that. I liked working for 2 hours, 4 hours a day, something like that. I didn't want to be forced to work 8 hours per day.

#2 MONEY — You need to have enough to live on, and ideally more. I wanted to make $100,000 or more. My initial goal was to cover my bill, move out of my parents' house, and cover my rent.

#3 DOING SOMETHING I WAS ACTUALLY PASSIONATE ABOUT — This was the last thing I eventually discovered. With the card site, I didn't have enough money from it, but I did have time freedom. It was not too much work, because it was when I was studying. I was passionate about the card game until I was 22."

At this point, he realized that he was growing up, and needed a new passion. What is key here is that his experiences dictated these three guidelines.

Gappers turn their experiences into principles. Take Harry Truman.

When he and his investors lost money in a Zinc mine, and later an Oil refinery, he was briefly despaired. Even when it turned out that they did not dig deep enough to find the millions of dollars of oil below, he would use this experience as a lesson for the future.

Harry Truman's ten years as a farmer shaped his principles. From rising early to working hard, he learned the values of a farmer.

Most people look at farming as a life of hard labor that you do for the rest of your life. Harry Truman saw it as a way to learn about the world. This comes down to principles.

However, principles are not abstract ideas. With the right message, you can spread your principles around the world.

Thomas Jefferson had a lifelong passion for learning. As a young boy, he devoured topics like Latin, Greek, French, Architecture, History, and Mathematics. These pursuits would later be part of the inspiration for the Declaration of Independence. Later when he was president, he would advance many scientific theories through the funding and leadership he provided to the sciences.

As Jefferson stated, "I was bold in the pursuit of knowledge, never fearing to follow truth and reason to whatever results they led, and bearding every authority which stood in their way."

Abraham Lincoln, while not having the same opportunities as a child as Thomas Jefferson, also loved books.

His love of law was a natural extension of his love of books. While he was a clerk in New Salem, he started reading law books. These books would become the foundation of his philosophy on government and leadership as he rose through the political ranks.

Doris Kearns, author of *Team of Rivals*, states, "Few of his colleagues experienced so solitary or steep a climb to professional proficiency [...]. What is more, Lincoln had no outlet for discourse [...] nor did Lincoln have the social advantages [...] or the connections." As he told an aspiring young lawyer looking for advice in 1855, "Get the books, and read and study them."

He would work all day, and then read long into the night.

Books are great for defining your principles. However, for some of us, we also we also learn from those around us. Albert Einstein is a great example of this method.

First, he received personal tutoring from Max Talmud, a family friend, who introduced Einstein to higher-level mathematics and scientific principles.

Later, using clubs that he founded with friends like the Olympia Academy, he kept his mind busy as they discussed science and philosophy on a regular basis. This group of friends would play a large role in his views on science and philosophy throughout his life.

Finally, we also define our principles based on our experiences, as mentioned above.

Zig Ziglar was not a born sales man. In fact, he struggled early on to bring in sales. Part of this was because he did not know enough about the sales process. He learned by experience. Sometimes those experiences were rough.

Zig was able to overcome initial shortcomings as a sales man by understanding how his attitude would determine whether he closed a sale or not.

Conversely, sometimes we get overconfident as well.

Andrew Carnegie, early in his career, spread out his investments in iron, railroads, telegraph, bridge building, and bond fund-raising. All these different ventures had an effect on his financial well-being.

According to his auto-biography, he decided it was better to "Put all good eggs in one basket, and then watch that basket."

I have no faith in the policy of scattering one's resources, and in my experience I have rarely if ever met a man who achieved preeminence in money-making-certainly never one in manufacturing-who was interested in many concerns."

Defining your principles does not come from one specific source. Instead, it is something that takes people a lifetime to figure out.

However, waiting your entire life to figure out what you want to do is a bit of a waste if you ask me. Therefore, we need to define your principles now. While it might not be perfect, it is better to have a work in progress than a STOP sign for your principles about life.

EXERCISE: DEFINE YOURSELF

To help you determine the best way to define your principles, let's look at the three main ways to figure your own principles?

1. **Education**
2. **Experiences**
3. **Relationships**

That is it. These are the three ways you define your principles for business and life. In some way or another, most things in life are the result of these three causes.

In many cases, you know your believes, but have let them become dormant. Like a muscle, you must continuously work out your principles, so they do not decay.

At the same time, remember your principles will change over time. This means that this exercise must not be done only once at the start of your business, but continuously as you grow.

Therefore, this section will not define your principles. Instead, you will mold them into your own guiding philosophy.

Look into your past, and see how your principles will define your business at this point in your life. Now either use the graphic below to write down how your experiences, education, and relationships have influenced your principles in life.

EDUCATION	EXPERIENCE	RELATIONSHIPS

Did your answers surprise you? How exactly did your education play a role in who you are today? Maybe it was more your experiences that define who you are. Perhaps your network of friends and family shaped your principles.

Start to construct a framework from your own personal beliefs, so you can build the type of business you deserve building.

Next, you need to spend time defining why you are in business. Think back to your month of activity. What made you happiest? Understand your why for becoming an entrepreneur.

To do this, use the questions at the end of this chapter as a way to determine the best way to define your business.

Questions give us the clarity that we need in business. They force us to think. Dedicate at least an hour to answering the questions below. Answer them to your satisfaction, and then move forward.

Defining your mission is not a race. Get it right! Understand your values and the business endeavor you are starting.

DEFINING QUESTIONS:

1. What makes your business unique?
2. What makes you unique? What are your special skills, talents, and ideas?
3. What experiences do you have that are unique to you?
4. How do you use those experiences in your new venture?
5. What is your vision for bettering this world?
6. What is your ideal client?
7. How will you help them?
8. Who are your competitors?
9. What makes you different from them?
10. What do they do better than you?

➡5. Help Along the Way

One of the things that inspired me to talk to Scarlett & Stephen Knuth was how they are the complete power couple. Most entrepreneurs separate their work and personal life, this photography couple combine every aspect of their life together.

Stephen stated, "We love sharing, and think that sharing is a huge part of leadership, because Scarlett and I will share things with each other. We are always talking, and always sharing."

Convincing your spouse to join you in your entrepreneurial endeavors is not required. The Knuth's know how to balance their personal and business life together.

As an entrepreneur you must focus on what skills you need on your team.

Anita Campbell is a great example of this philosophy. When she bought BizSugar she said, "I think my greatest accomplishment is providing employment for a team and numerous freelancers. We have five employees on the team, including a few family members. We also have eighteen different freelancers who work for us regularly either as staff writers or paid editors on Small Business Trends, our moderator team, or our BizSugar social media team.

When you can provide employment for other people, it's a very gratifying thing."

Anita said, "I'm really gratified to provide that employment. I just get a lot of positive energy back from that."

Carol Tice had a similar philosophy.

"It is more about work life balance for me. Drawing lines about when I am not on and not available. The one thing I can do that no one else on my team can, is have these experts create these boot camps, and mentor them.

I am trying to outsource a lot of other stuff. Managing the business is a big challenge now with over 1100 members.

I thought 1,000 would be an upper limit, where it could not possibly grow. My webmasters were like no. Then I thought at some point, won't it seem too anonymous. I have a large moderator staff. It is not just me answering questions.

I have four to five pro writers at my level, who are moderators. Then a lot of volunteer moderators, who get a free membership for moderating and helping out."

However, as many who have attempted to build a solid team already know, it is not always rosy.

David Meerman Scott's biggest challenge was sticking to his principles long enough to retrain the team around him.

"I had to stick to my convictions. That was difficult at times, because I was a kind of a lone voice out there. I was always advocating that you should distribute valuable content on the web for free with no registration.

Things like a white paper. For a long time people had been putting white papers out on the marketplace in exchange for an email address. My strategy was make the white paper completely free, because that will spread your ideas as people share your content.

I really had to stick to that conviction, because 95% of people would say that I was wrong, and they would adamantly argue with me about why I was wrong."

One of my favorite examples of bringing together a great team comes from President Abraham Lincoln.

In the 1860 Republican primary election, Lincoln defeated the expected presidential front-runners: William Seward, Edward Bates, and Edwin Stanton.

When he became president, he asked each of his primary opponents to become secretaries in his cabinet. Here we have the greatest president in history. Now we know why. He did not care about winning. Lincoln cared about building a coalition that would keep the nation together.

His principles were so strong, that at the time of his death, Seward considered him his closest friend and Bates sadly stated, "Now he belongs to the ages."

EXERCISE: TEAM BUILDING

People come together for a principle, an idea.

When you define yourself in the previous chapter, you are by extension, defining your team and partners.

In the beginning this might be weird, but it is true.

When I was in real estate, I did not have the right team, because I did not believe in what I was doing. Those same reasons helped me create a successful online marketing agency. Be mindful of whom you work with in business.

WHEN BUILDING A TEAM YOU NEED TO KEEP THESE IDEAS IN MIND

First, do you trust this person? I've been in partnerships, which failed despite the amazing opportunity we had.

You have to be able to trust your gut feeling, and see if this person is the right for your venture. Do they complement you?

Trust your instincts. Use the principles you came devised, because they will be your guide to finding the right team.

Second, start small. Some of the best partnerships I've ever had started with a simple step years earlier.

Most entrepreneurs think a partnership is all or nothing. Not true! Start small. Then expand the next time.

Third, always keep looking for the right one. Finding good team members is like dating. You always want to look your best, and you want to know how many fish are in the sea. You never know which one is going to be your princess or prince charming partner.

TEAM BUILDING QUESTIONS

1. Whom do you trust in your life now?
2. Why do you trust them?
3. What is the number one thing a new team member/partner must possess to work with you?
4. What do you not want in team members?
5. Can you see working with them one year from now? Two years? Five years? Ten years?

➡6. Motivation

Zig Ziglar used to say, "Motivation is like bathing, you have to do it every day." The first time I heard that line I laughed, because it was funny. The second time I heard this line I laughed, because I lost my motivation for what I was doing. The third time I heard this line I laughed, because it was true.

You must always motivate yourself. Do not expect to wake up suddenly one day motivated, ready to face the rest of your life. Each day, you must look at how to stay motivated that day. Think about what you have, and what you want. Then use that motivation in whatever you do.

Sometimes that motivation will be a great ideal you strive to reach. Other times, it will be something quantifiable.

David Oldenburg discussed his motivation as follow.

"If you're good at what you do, and you really work it you're going to make a lot of money. I knew if I stayed on as a paramedic that I was never going to make more than $20 an hour. That was fine when I was in my 20s, but at a certain point you want to buy a decent house, you want to send your kids to college, and it's hard to do on $20 an hour. That was my drive. Truthfully, it was money. I wanted to make more."

David Meerman Scott on the other hand had a vision for his life that motivated him to keep going.

"What always kept me going is I never want to work for somebody else again. I wanted to live by my wits, running my own business."

As you can see, motivation is what you make of it. For David Oldenburg he saw a chance for financial freedom.

While David Meerman Scott wanted that as well, he wanted to avoid working in a traditional job.

However, motivation is not just about financial freedom.

Gerry Oginski had a simple motivation that propelled his business.

"When I started to get those calls, I realized that people needed this information. The motivation was that I am at the forefront; no one else is doing this. In fact, I was the first attorney in the country who used educational videos to present this information."

He saw his opportunity as a responsibility to share with others information he possessed.

Yet sometimes, our internal motivation is enough. Take Carol Tice.

"I don't have motivation problems. I have calm down and go watch a movie problem. I come from a money worrying kind of family, and I was always wondering how I would be financially secure.

My dad was an independent insurance agent. I watched him hustle clients, selling the hardest product there is; except for cemetery plots. He worked 18 hours per day to make that happen. He would eat dinner with us, and then drive out to make night calls. My sister and I both have a huge drive, and he taught us that girls could do whatever they want with themselves …

My webmaster said to me the other day, 'Oh my god! I looked into your WordPress editorial calendar, and am just blown away by how many blog post titles are in here. I have ideas coming out of my rear all the time that I can't wait to put up on my blog. Some new thought, angle approach, or market that I can tell them about."

Personally, I believe that none of us can accomplish massive success by ourselves. The idea of a self-made man is a misnomer that holds no truth in today's society.

Steve Olsher had this interesting insight about motivation, with a keen understanding of how we grow as entrepreneurs.

"When you create a new site, for the most part you're like this looks really good. This is what I want. This captures the essence. Then a year later, something else comes up technology wise. Or you get a different vision, or whatever it might be, and you recreate the site. You get the new site up, you look back at the old site, and you go that old site kind of sucked. Then you do it again a year later and you look back and say — you know that old site really wasn't that good, but at the time you're like this is great.

In terms of how I look at my life and what keeps me motivated if you will, it's to achieve the unachievable, which is to get to that point of where everything is the way I want it to be. As you know that's never going to happen. It's an illusion. An imaginary line in the sand we draw. Once we reach it, we just move the line farther.

I think that's what keeps me motivated. Knowing that I can serve more people, knowing that my teaching can improve, and my speaking and interviewing can improve. I know there are people out there who are waiting for me. That's what keeps me motivated.

One of my coaching clients Andrea said that it took her sixty years to realize that she's the solution to someone else's problem. That's what really keeps me motivated. I know I am the solution to someone else's problem."

Motivation, like many of the other concepts we discuss here is an elusive idea. You need to discover your motivation on your own, which is what we want you to do with the exercise in this chapter.

EXERCISES: MOTIVATION BUILDERS

Often when people talk about motivation, it seems like this big mysterious thing that falls out of the sky one day to help you achieve your dreams. However, motivation does not work that way.

Instead, you constantly have to work at the motivation you find is right for you. While everyone's motivation is different, we want to examine a few ways to increase your motivation.

First, review your work in Chapter 3 about defining your goals. Defining what you want out of life. When you know what you want, the rest becomes easier. This is one of the first steps to increasing your motivation when you are in the gap. You need a cause, something to fight for greater than yourself.

Second, break down your goals into smaller steps that you take every day. We do that by looking at your KPI's (Key Performance Indicators) that you need to focus on each day to reach your goals.

Motivation is great for keeping you going. However, this is where we need you to start creating meaningful actions to bring your motivations to reality. To do this, you need to understand what steps you take every day.

Before we go further, I want to give a shout out to my coach, James Budd, who is always on me about my KPI's. Below, is a blank sample spreadsheet to show you how I created my first KPI's.

	SALES			WEEKLY AND MONTHLY SALESPERSON ACTIVITY		
	Week Sales	Month Sales			Activity 1	Activity 2
Services						
				TIME SPENT		
				Weekly		
				Monthly		
Coaching						
				NEW CONNECTION		
				Weekly		
Total				Monthly		

Third, track your actions. Once you have everything set up, then you need to make sure that you commit to these goals. I know this is one of the hardest things for me to do. I find it very laborious. This is not a book about resources.

Check out our free companion eBook *101 Free Tools Online — http://startupgap. com/101-free-online-tools* if you need some free online resources.

However, this is the one part of the book, where I want to address a few software programs to help you stay organized.

- **Trello** — This is like a free post-it note site. Great for organizing your thoughts across a team environment. If you want to see an expert at work with Trello, connect with Gail Gardner at GrowMap.Com.
- **Insightly** — CRM and Project Manager rolled into one, which is rare for a product that is free for a single user.
- **Freshbooks** — This is great for invoicing, and accounting help, as well as project management.
- **Basecamp** — Do you want project management software with cloud storage? Then this is your solution.

We will discuss more about keeping on top of your business consistently in the next chapter on Habits. For now, we need to focus on how to keep track of our goals, so we are motivated to keep moving forward. Using this software, you get a first glimpse of how far you have come over time.

Fourth, when I do this I need to reward myself. Motivation is not just about big, long-term goals. Whenever you stick to your goals, treat yourself. Whether it is by taking your spouse out for a nice dinner, or just buying that marketing software you wanted, it does not matter. The key is to congratulate yourself on the small accomplishments; so you are even more motivated to reach the bigger ones.

Fifth, conversely do not be hard on yourself if you falter. Most people get really motivated when they first start, but falter at a certain point. Just because you fell behind one week or one day does not mean you should stop. Redouble your efforts and keep going.

Consistency is everything in business and in life. I started writing my blog in 2010. My goal was to blog five days a week for one year. Three years later, I had almost 1,000 blog posts on my site.

In fact, if not for that one blog, you would not be reading this book today. (Whether that is a good thing or not, I am not sure. *If good, make sure to review us with 5 stars on Amazon and GoodReads.*

Here is the link to the Amazon page: *http://startupgap.com/amazon)*

Sixth, understand how you work. I am sure in some corner of the world, some super human people work 18 hours a day without break, and still go strong 7 days a week, year in and year out. However, I am not among them.

Personally, I work best in the mornings and late afternoon/early evenings. The other times of the day, I am not at pique shape to help my business.

Everyone has their own rhythm. Determine what works best for you. If you have been stuck in a corporate environment, this might seem radical. However, 9 to 5 is not exactly a smart way to do business. Most people cannot perform at their best for 8 hours straight; 45-minute lunch breaks be damned!

UNDERSTANDING YOUR MOTIVATION

In the end, you will find your motivation over time. Writing down your list of motivations will help, but what I found is that as I continued to work, I learned more and more about what truly motivated me. The more I work, the more motivated I am to succeed. This partially explains the *Start Up Gap*.

Most entrepreneurs come in with vague motivations, and have to mold them into something more. Going through the six steps above not only helps you understand your motivations, but also how to mold your motivation into a workable business that can deliver on your dreams.

Consider Dwan Twyford, who we profile later in the book, for a second. She was a single mother with a baby, who had 90 days to make her business work. That is a level of motivation most of us do not have.

While your motivation may not be that pressing, you probably have something that drives you.

MOTIVATION QUESTIONS

1. What motivates you to do more?
2. What generally gets in your way?
3. What times of the day do you get the most done?
4. How good are you at setting (and completing) goals?
5. What is the biggest challenge for achieving your goals?

➡7. Habits of the Greats

Malcolm Gladwell says to become an expert it takes 10,000 hours. To get there, you need to be consistent. Without good habits, you will have trouble managing your time. Habits provide a schedule for you to focus on the important.

While every Gapper had their own suggestion, most of them managed their time, so they could reach their goals. Here are some of the habit secrets they discovered that made a difference.

Joel Comm said, "Keep going! Try to innovate. Do cool stuff. I like to do things that people have not done before. A lot of people look at what is successful and then they duplicate that. I don't think that is the answer. The answer is to be an original."

The power of habit is that you can determine your habits now, so you can get the most out of your business.

Leonardo da Vinci spent time everyday living creatively. He would always strive to think out of the box. It was this habitual practice that enabled him to come up with paintings, ideas, and machines that were so advanced they would not be created for another 500 years (airplane, tank, etc.)

You can also spend time each day reflecting on your life.

Liz Strauss "started taking photographs of the sunrise over the lake, because it gives me something to get up for every day. Right now, I will probably take a couple of shots of sunset, because the sky has all sorts of colors.

I have this incredible experience of seeing all the colors of the lake. Doing something artistic, and uploading them to Instagram. Getting all these people saying, 'wow! That is awesome! I live for your photographs.' I get to experience the photographs a second time, and I get to say thank you, thank you, thank you.

It is an incredible experience to start your day saying thank you for an hour every day."

Zig Ziglar felt you need to "give a bit each day to those around you. You can have anything you want in the world as long as you help enough people achieve their goals." Each day, Zig was committed to helping millions of sales people around the world achieve their goal.

Jeff Bussas believes "The greatest habit you can have is to keep reading. I try to fit in an hour or two a day. That includes books, as well as blogs. I'm innately curious so that helps.

Stephen King's talked about continual education this way. "If you want to write a lot, read a lot. There's no mystery to it."

Habit is that irritating thing that scares you away from starting, and terrifies you from stopping. It is the boring things you do every day, as you start your journey between dreams and success. The true gap happens when you bore people with your day long enough to become gifted at what you do.

The challenge with habits is that it constant focus and clarity is needed. This means the work that we did earlier on motivation and defining your principles will make it easier for you to maintain the habits of success.

EXERCISE: HABIT BUILDING

When we were writing the *Start Up Gap*, we conducted a number of surveys. The number one challenge most people had was time management. Habits improve your time management. Here are some strategies for improving your habits on a daily basis:

First, have a weekly and monthly plan. Base this on the mission you created in Chapter 3 on defining your principles.

Second, focus on your plan first thing in the morning. Review your plan in the morning, so you have a plan. This does not have to be formal. I work out most mornings, and go through my day in my head. Then check my Trello board to make sure that I did not miss anything.

Third, write down your daily action. Once you have your plan, write it down before you forget. Going back to the Trello board idea I cited before, move projects around based on what needs to get finished today. I use due dates to increase urgency.

Fourth, turn off all distractions. Unless your job requires you to be on the phone, turn it off. When you meet clients, turn off all distractions. Be focused and present in the moment.

Fifth, time yourself. I like 15 minute time chunks, because it forces me to be alert and work fast, yet effectively. Also, statistically most people cannot stay focused for more than 15 minutes at a time.

More to the point, I then use Parkinson's Law. This states that time constraints improve the importance of the work. This means, if you give yourself 1 hour to complete each task, it is not as important. However, if you give yourself 15 minutes, then you will have only enough time to focus on the task.

HABIT QUESTIONS

1. What good habits do you have?
2. What bad habits do you have?
3. How do you develop positive habits?
4. How do you reward yourself for good habits?
5. Can you do this every day for the next year? Two years? Five years? Ten years?

➡8. The Story of Success

What story do you tell yourself? How do you portray yourself in these stories? Are you a gallant hero rescuing maidens? Perhaps you are a modern day Wall Street trader making it big in the Big Apple? Are you a modern savior with ideas that will change the world?

How you view yourself is important. While many people will see you as a success or failure from the beginning, it is your own understanding of yourself that determines how far you go.

As Henry Ford once said, "If you think you can or think you can't, you're right."

Understanding your own story is crucial to the *Start Up Gap*. As we discussed in breaking down the numbers in Chapter 1, 45% of the Gappers' main challenge was that people were negative towards their as they started on their journey.

While the Gappers overcame this adversity, we find many more do not. Consider the study published by **Psychtests.com.**

According to the study, 66% of people when criticized or fail, are overly hard on themselves. The majority of people have trouble accepting criticism and moving on. However, using that criticism as a source of energy and passion can help you.

This is why every day when you are in your own gap, you need to focus on your own success story. Your vision of yourself must be stronger than the critics.

Liz Strauss has the idea. "I get up at about 4:30 AM, and I feel successful by about 10 in the morning.

It's an everyday thing. One day you think you own the world, and the next you think your house is about to fall down."

Success is not a one-time event that follows you for the rest of your life. Instead, it is the daily grind of making sure you do better than the day before.

Chef Dennis Littley espoused this belief.

"I think success is measured in small steps, with a lot of small steps along the way where I feel I was successful. You have to have those small goals, those easily attainable goals to measure your success."

Steve Olsher did not believe that success was something he ever reached. He calls success insignificant; yet I would call his believe the reason behind his passion to excel.

"My book hit the *New York Times* list, and I never stopped to celebrate. I think a lot of that is from a very young age I guess I felt insignificant, and no matter what I was able to do, even on the business front, if I could attain enough material significance that would somehow squash the feeling of insignificance that I felt.

The bottom line for me is that even to this day that feeling of insignificance is still pervasive. Even though my contributions have helped thousands of people, I still believe that I haven't reached enough people and I still believe that there is more work to do.

So I just can't say this is where I want to be and I've reached it because as I've said that place just doesn't exist for me."

While many of the entrepreneurs we talked to are not satisfied with their success, many have a vision of what this success looks like.

For example, Carol Tice said, "my theory was that if it could grow to 300 people, the *membership* could kind of gel. Trying to remember how long it took to do that. Maybe 6 months. My business plan was that if I worked really, really hard it would have 500

START UP GAP   27

members and solve all my financial problems."

Yaro Starak described, "A mind shift change after the Entrepreneurs Journey course had settled down. I had to make sure it was a great program. Then in 2008, I travelled the world for 8 months.

Things kept going, but what changed about me was I saw how I used my time differently.

For example, I would never worry about spending money on incidental things anymore. I would never get annoyed that I had to pay for dinner, or that someone used something else. Or I bought an expensive meal. I realized that I get much more leverage from using my time in a few core things. SO, DON'T GET UPSET WITH THE LITTLE STUFF."

Success can change you or empower you to do more. It also allows you to reflect on how far you have gone.

The power of the different Gappers to reach success still astounds me. I hear many of their stories, and feel a bit of awe and excitement thinking about what they accomplished.

That made me realize why I wrote the book. I want to make sure you understand the value of their stories.

Some people will read this as an inspiration. Others will find the lessons in the stories. Finally, many will find the answer to turn their own story into a success.

Whatever the case is, this chapter helps you put everything we have discussed for the previous six steps together perspective. Everything about success requires you to get there in your mind, long before it really happens.

EXERCISE: SUCCESS REQUIRES PREPARATION

This entire conversation has been leading up to one inevitable point. Success is not a matter of luck, but of preparation. By using the other steps we discussed, you are well on your way.

However, we still have a few more things that we need to do. Specifically, you need to make sure that you are always continuing to build relationships.

Additionally, maintain your focus as you grow. Growing your business is what every company strives for over the years.

This is why it is important as you grow and succeed that you keep in mind why your reached for something more.

The moment you forget and lose your focus, is the moment when your success can turn to failure.

Therefore, for this chapter, the exercise is for you to write your *Start Up Gap* story.

Here are a few elements to include in the story, along with the sample story (below) I created for myself for this exercise.

1. Include in your story the first six steps: actions, challenges, principles, teams, motivation, and habits.
2. Write the story as if it were a journal to your future self, so you can remember where you were today.
3. Go from dreams to success. This can be something that happened, or you plan to happen.

4. Be open and honest with yourself. Unless you are publishing this story, no one else will read it.
5. Remember your story in adversity. Remember your story in success.

MY STORY

A little over 13 months ago, I had a shimmer of a vision for a book. One that was so audacious that it scared me to even consider it. The book was a complete departure from every project I had previously worked on before.

It would also require me to re-learn a lot of the skills for my current business. The book was called *Start Up Gap*.

I was still writing the final pages of my latest book, eMarketing Experience, when the idea came to me. Since I needed to finish my first book, I did the only sensible thing at the time. I bought the domain *StartUpGap.com*, and turned it into a website.

A few days later, I wrote the first draft in what would become the opening chapter for this book. However, before I could start I had a huge challenge. No one really understood why I was not talking about social media and blogging anymore. That was after all, why they came to me for advice.

"Did you stop blogging," they asked. "What happened to your blog *AndyNathan. Net*," they inquired? I assured everyone that I still helped businesses with their online marketing. That just confused people more.

So, I set about defining what and why I was writing the book *Start Up Gap*. It would contain in it my principles for helping entrepreneurs improve their business. Understanding how, as I called them at the time, The Greats, really started their business. It is so important for me to be able to explain how understanding exactly what they achieved is beneficial for others to apply to build their own business.

For the first three months that I worked on *Start Up Gap*, I went about promoting everything by myself. That was when I realized that I just could not handle my current work load for clients, and write the weekly blog posts for *Start Up Gap* at the same time.

I hired a virtual assistant, Candace Chira, in Chicago who has been a lifesaver. She is able to pick up the slack where I do not have the time or energy to do everything myself.

As I neared the end of writing the book; however, tragedy struck. My grandfather, Mel Gurewitz, died. I saw him in the hospital two days before he passed.

Unfortunately we were not really able to have a last conversation, because his situation deteriorated so quickly.

I dedicated this book to him, so we can finally have a final conversation. Whenever I wavered on finishing the book, I look at a picture of him in my office.

Then every day I did a little more to complete the book; as well as a few power sessions at Starbucks. Note: Thank you for the Starbucks card, which gives me unlimited free refills on tea. My apologies to Starbucks shareholders for the slight dip in revenue last quarter.

As I am almost finished with the book, I see the day where I speak in front of a crowd talking about the power of the *Start Up Gap*. Book in hand, I read a passage, and inspire entrepreneurs to do more with their life. A young entrepreneur looks up, and finally gets it. Mission Accomplished!

Andy

SUCCESS QUESTIONS

1. How do you treat your best customers?
2. What do you to help your referral partners?
3. What is your focus in business?
4. Do you believe in yourself?
5. When did you feel most successful in your life? Why?

➡9. Stories of the Greats (Case Studies)

We spent the first part of this book discussing how to become successful. While we interspersed some of the tales of the entrepreneurs and leaders that we have profiled over the past year, I think we need to talk about the stories that influenced this book.

After all, the stories are a core component of *Start Up Gap.*

Understanding what really happened between the initial dream and success is not possible without digging into these stories.

Therefore, the second part of the book will break down the principles and ideas into case studies of the entrepreneurs we have profiled.

These case studies are the stories of how they bridged the gap. I did my best to convey everything through their words directly here, because I do not like cutting out Gappers quotes. However, to clarify some points, you will see my commentary interspersed as well.

➡️Here's The Story: Joel Comm

BIO

Joel Comm is an Internet pioneer, New York Times Best-selling author, Internationally-known speaker, serial entrepreneur and New Media Marketing Strategist.

A lot of people look at what is successful and then they duplicate that. I don't thing that is the answer. The answer is to be an original.

Joel Comm

THE DREAM

Joel started out with a simple goal, not a dream. He wanted to get free video games. As an avid player, he thought it would be cool to start up a gaming magazine so he could receive and review the free games. This was the start of ClassicGames.Com, which he later sold to Yahoo! for millions.

THE CHALLENGE

He received $25,000 in angel investing to start out the business. However, by the beginning of 1996, "was down to about a dollar in my bank account. It was scary…which begs the question what happened … Here's the thing; I knew what I built was good, and that the web was going somewhere. This is where I turned to my faith in a big way. I literally turned to prayer, and said, *I quit my job. There is not enough money coming in, I thought this would work. God I really thought this is what you wanted me to do. If you want me to do this, show me a sign and literally drop money in from the sky.*"

About a week later, he received an email from a Japanese conglomerate that he never heard of, and I do not even think I could spell out correctly. They offered to pay him $5000 per month to re-purpose his content for their site. This was the turning point in his business.

THE ACTIONS

Here is Joel's recipe for success in three easy steps.

ACTION ONE-HAVE FAITH

When times were tough, he "turned to my faith in a big way. Literally turned to prayer, and said I quit my job, there is not enough money coming in, I thought this would work. God I really thought this is what you wanted me to do. If you want me to do this, show me a sign and literally drop money in from the sky."

ACTION TWO-INNOVATE

"Keep going! Try to innovate. Do cool stuff. I like to do things that people have not done before... A lot of people look at what is successful and then they duplicate that. I don't think that is the answer. The answer is to be an original."

ACTION THREE-EMBRACE CHANGE

Stay ahead of the curve! Thinking about innovation, we also need to look at the fact that he embraced the web much earlier than most people did. He would later embrace Google Ads and iPhones apps earlier as well. All of this was of tremendous use, because he was not stuck in yesterday's thought processes.

FINAL THOUGHTS

Joel's story to me is amazing. He saw the opportunity of the internet long before most of us ever did. Some of the cool things he did while starting his business in the 90⊠s might seem commonplace now, but were ahead of their time when he started.

➡️Here's The Story: Dan Antonelli

BIO

Dan Antonelli is the President and Creative Director of a successful, award-winning 15-person design studio, Graphic D-Signsm Inc for past 19 years. Author of three logo design books on small business branding, including his newly released third book 'Building a Big Small Business Brand'.

You never really reach a point whwere you say you made it. I live by the motto that everything I did today, tomorrow I want to do a little bit better.

Dan Antonelli

THE DREAM

Dan worked in high school at a sign shop, where his burgeoning talents demonstrated his interest in sign painting. As he neared graduation, he told his parents that he wanted to turn his passion into a career as a sign painter. They told him no.

He was told to go to college, and said OK, "graphic design is obviously somewhat related to Communications, and I will learn about advertising and graphic design."

The funny thing was that University of Scranton was the wrong school for a budding designer, because it was more of a liberal arts school — not a graphic design school. However, this worked out in his favor, because he got a lot of hands on experience through internships, and also learned the marketing side of the industry — which most creatives never experience because of where they went to school.

Upon graduation, he found a job in NYC as a designer. But he missed working with businesses like he used to working in the sign shop. So at the age of 25, he launched his company, working nights and weekends while maintaining his day job. In two years, he'd quit his day job and go full-time.

"In the beginning, I was happy to be doing something that I loved, and was less focused on the business side, which is not uncommon for creatives. A few years after starting, however, my wife was pregnant, she was on bed rest, and she couldn't work anymore. All that security was going away and I needed to look at this like a business….and chart a course for the future, and what I wanted to be doing, and how to best get there.

His schooling helped give him the tools to do this.

THE CHALLENGE

It was scary when he made the jump to quit his full time job as a designer working for someone else to launch his business, "because no one in my family had ever started a business before. There were no entrepreneurs on either side of my family. My father worked for the Port Authority of New York & New Jersey which is a big government agency. His father worked for the post office. My other grandfather worked for the federal government. So, no one quit a good job to be an entrepreneur."

THE ACTIONS

Dan's recipe for success is as follows.

ACTION ONE-BE OBSESSIVE

"Be obsessive about you discipline to the point where it probably annoys your family and most of the people you know. You cannot substitute that type of passion towards a specific discipline. Be a sponge — learn everything you can about your passion. Reach out to people you admire, engage them in conversations about how they got to where they are."

ACTION TWO – DO A LITTLE BETTER TOMORROW

"You never really reach a point where you say you made it. I live by the motto that everything I did today, tomorrow I want to do a little bit better. Since day one, that's been our agency's philosophy. I stop and marvel at our best work, but I also know, tomorrow, we'll do something even better. Never rest on your laurels, or get complacent in the mastering of your craft."

ACTION THREE-MASTER YOUR CRAFT

Master your craft. So often, people jump around too much in business. Dan has focused on graphic design, since he was in college. While, he made adjustments as the economy changed, he still focuses on design, and branding as his specific niche. As a person obsessed with logos and brands, he built an entire agency around the notion that branding is the single most important asset for any small business.

FINAL THOUGHTS

Follow your passions, because you are never sure where they will take you in life. Dan Antonelli has embodied this in whatever he worked on for his business.

➡Here's The Story: Amy Baxter

BIO

Dr. Amy Baxter founded Buzzy 4 Shots in 2006 to prevent personal pain for children taking shots. She is also does medical researcher, runs a pediatric emergency practice, and has a husband and three kids under the age of 17!

If you have something you can make a prototype of, then put up a Craigslist ad. If no one bites, then probably not worth derailing your life.

Amy Baxter

THE DREAM

"I knew that I needed a quick pain reliever back in 2001 when my son, now 16, was four. I had the idea in 2004, and then finally decided to commit to a company in 2006."

The idea was Buzzy, which is a vibrator that comes with a custom cooling patch to help numb the pain of shots, as well as pains you have in your back and other parts of your body.

THE CHALLENGE

"I think that we are so convinced of our brilliance and our own ideas that as soon as we tell the right person, they are going to hand us a check for $1 million and we are not going to have to do any work. The first few years I told people selectively, and waited for people to take the bait. No one did.

I decided that maybe I need to develop the product a little, and then someone would buy it. So, I patented it myself … thought how hard can this be, I will learn patent law. Went to a patent attorney after I did the structure and bones, and they made it ship shape…

After the patent, waited for someone to dangle a million dollars, and they didn't. I thought maybe they need to see it … I had neighbors donate old cell phones, so I could use the vibrators…too big…they would not work, but was able to use the coin motors…

I went to some design firms…and I was like 'Do you WANT TO SEE MY BUZZY,' and then I showed them my idea. Figured that they would be interested in buying it for one million dollars.

No one bought, so I figured I will have to go ahead and do this…One of the design firms understood it enough, because one of the principals had open heart surgery as a kid. He got it…They took the project on as a side bar."

THE ACTIONS

Here is Amy's recipe for success

ACTION ONE – USE HARO

"I look at HARO (Help A Reporter Out), I habitually look at the PR opportunities, rather than outsourcing it. I am good at writing, and no one knows my story as good as I do. It is not sexy, but that is where I apply leverage."

Real quick! Key words here are no one knows your story as well as you do. Great way to know what to outsource, and what to do yourself in business.

ACTION TWO – KEEP IN TOUCH

"I am really good at keeping in touch with people I met someplace before. I highly recommend in your entrepreneurial notebook keeping pages of business cards. I arrange them temporally, and this is all from one business conference. When I want to get in touch with people from that conference, they are all right here."

ACTION THREE – KEEP GOING

Don't stop at the first sign of trouble. Amy's story about how she just assumed someone would buy the product for a million dollars is a perfect example. She understands that people do not buy untested ideas. They buy proven products.

As she says, "No one steals an idea, people steal a finished product. You might not want to tell people in your industry without a patent. There is no reason not to tell friends and family. If they do not encourage you then it is probably not worth it."

FINAL THOUGHTS

"It's scommitment. If you are going to be an entrepreneur, especially with things like Shark Tank, and with things that make being an entrepreneur exciting.

To be a good entrepreneur you have to really commit. You have to know that it is a decade of hard work. You have to accept that you are going to be the cheerleader of your product to the detriment of your friendships…You can't put it down when you go home…if you are awake you are at work."

➡Here's The Story: Kristi Hines

BIO

Kristi Hines is a freelance writer, ghostwriter, and professional blogger. Since 2010, she has provided high-quality blog content to many brands, businesses, and publications including American Express, Bigcommerce, Capital One, FreshBooks, HubSpot, KISSmetrics, Search Engine Watch, and Social Media Examiner.

 You have to say this is my business.

You have to be the boss of yourself, and kick your own butt.

Kristi Hines

THE DREAM

"I started blogging in 2008. It kind of evolved into a career. I had my own personal blog, and got interested in the marketing side. Then had a few clients who wanted to pay me."

That is smart marketing. Do not look for clients instead fill a need. Many businesses need writers to create dynamic content for them, because they do not know how to do so (or do not want to spend their time writing.) A great niche!

"I always loved writing, even from high school. Enjoyed writing ¬¬¬papers and things like that. I was doing online marketing consulting for an agency, and even while I was doing that, I enjoyed writing about the process, even more than actually doing it. When I was invited by my first client, it seemed like a perfect fit."

THE CHALLENGE

"My biggest challenge was that I was working a full time job 40 hours per week, and then doing a freelance writing on the side. It was hard for me to find that really perfect time to say, "OK, let's switch over, I am going to be my own employer. I always was instilled with the idea that a 9-5 job is what you are supposed to do."

When Kristi mentioned this, it reminded me of Amy Baxter last week discussing how she was working as a pediatric doctor while starting Buzzy. Also, Dan Antonelli had a similar challenge when starting his agency.

THE ACTIONS

Kristi's Recipe for success

ACTION ONE-KICK YOUR BUTT INTO ACTION

"You have to say this is my business. You have to be the boss of yourself, and kick your own butt."

As an entrepreneur that is the hardest thing to do. You sometimes just have to "will" yourself to start. No one is there to tell you to do it. You just have to make it happen. Then when you start, sometimes you cannot stop until you are finished. Momentum is everything.

ACTION TWO-THIS IS YOUR CAREER

"When I first started, I never thought of freelancing as a career. I thought of it as a side income, I put the title in my by-line."

Amazing how some of the most inspired thoughts come from simple ideas. Something like, maybe I should add freelancer to my by-line. Tell people what you do, or they will probably never guess it.

ACTION THREE-LIVING PORTFOLIO

"I have been very fortunate that I had a lot of clients reaching out to me. My first client was the jumping point for that. All my work is public, so I have a living portfolio where new clients find me. And they say, I see what you did for them, can you do this for us."

However, we did go on to discuss how, "most of it has been the internal nervousness, like what happens if content marketing goes dead tomorrow."

"Right now I have been trying to be more productive. Like focusing when I am writing. Close down my email, and turn off Facebook. Actually have a program on Chrome called STAY FOCUSED to keep me off Buzzfeed and sites like this."

FINAL THOUGHTS

This is a story on focus and passion. By figuring out how you can be paid for what you love doing, you can find a niche where people will want your services for the skills you provide. Discovering that is at the heart of every venture, which is why there is normally a gap between the dream and the success. Entrepreneurs are using this time to determine how they can best help others with their knowledge and powers. Kristi Hines figured out that her power was writing.

➡Here's The Story: Stephen and Scarlett Knuth

BIO

Scarlett & Stephen are husband & wife luxury wedding photographers based in Nashville, TN. Together, their work has been seen on TLC's Wedding Day Makeover television show, ABC's 20/20 and Good Morning America, in publications such as Grace Ormonde's Wedding Style, The Knot, Southern Weddings, Weddings Unveiled, Weddings Illustrated and voted one of the Best Of Weddings for photography studios by The Knot Magazine.

Note: After the interview with them, Stephen received an amazing offer in telecom that was too good to pass up.

We love sharing and think that sharing is a huge part of leadership.

Scarlett & Stephen Knuth

THE DREAM

Stephen — "My journey began as a filmmaker.

Of course, you have a family member getting married, and they said, 'Hey! We have a photographer, but not a videographer, can you help us out.' I said, 'sure.' I did their wedding video, and edited it the same way I would edit a movie.

From that first wedding, they had friends who were getting married, who came to me and said, 'I would love to have you do my wedding video."

… Something happened to me in the dark room. I fell in love with it, being in the fixer, with the chemicals all over my hands. Then I told my film making clients that I was a photographer. That started the business."

Scarlett-" I got into photography for the romance.

After college, I got into that phase where all of my friends started getting married. Similar to Stephen's background, they had a photographer, but needed a videographer. It started at first like, I could film your wedding, I could edit ¬¬on iVideo.

After about a year of doing videography, I decide I was attracted to the photography side of it too."

THE CHALLENGE

Scarlett — "OK I have this love for photography, and I have this love for love stories. How do I take this passion that I have, and make it into a profitable, sustainable business.' Especially in this industry, most photographers are just part-time, and I knew it was something I wanted to be a full-time business.

My dad was an entrepreneur, and I saw what he was able to do with taking a business, and growing it into something incredible. I was very inspired by that, and I was lucky to have him before he passed away. He was a great mentor, and guided me along the way!"

Stephen — "For me, my dad is very successful in business, and I am surrounded by a family of entrepreneurs who are successful at what they do. They inspired me; however, I was also looking at the challenges of this. They did this in different fields."

THE ACTIONS

The Knuth's recipe for success

ACTION ONE-READ, READ, AND READ

"I read books all the time. I love reading. I work like a crazy animal. I work all day long, and I listen to audio books as I work. I have Google Docs open, and then pause and take a note. Books are a fantastic tool."

ACTION TWO-GET BACK TO PEOPLE QUICKLY

"Making a habit of getting back to people in an efficient time, and not making them sit and wait forever. I think about when I got started, and I reached out to a photographer that I admired respond back to me four months later, and I thought, 'that was rude.'"

ACTION THREE-HAVE A GOOD TEAM

"This might sound obvious, but have a good team around you. We discussed this in the team section, but with a husband and wife photography team, you get a lot of integrated work together. They trust each other, and are there to help each other build the business."

FINAL THOUGHTS

Stephen's point about how he challenged himself to reach the goals of the top-level people in their industry was telling of their *Start Up Gap*.

My takeaway from talking to this amazing power couple is that the power of team work is essential in how they operate. Every step of the way, Scarlett & Stephen are communicating about how to improve their business. As entrepreneurs, we always talk about having the right team around us. Having your spouse as your business partner creates a level of trust that most entrepreneurs would love to have in their business.

➡Here's The Story: David Meerman Scott

BIO

Leading Marketing and Sales Speaker for Companies and at Conferences Worldwide. His 2007 book "The New Rules of Marketing & PR" opened people's eyes to the new realities of marketing and public relations on the Web. Now in it's 4th edition, the book has sold 350,000 copies and is published in 25 languages from Arabic to Vietnamese.

David's other international bestsellers include "Real-Time Marketing & PR," "Newsjacking". He's co-author of "Marketing Lessons from the Grateful Dead" (written with HubSpot CEO Brian Halligan) and "Marketing the Moon" (written with Richard Jurek and with a foreword from Gene Cernan, the last man on the moon).

He serves on the advisory boards of HubSpot, GrabCAD, ExpertFile, VisibleGains, GutCheck, the Grateful Dead Archive at UC Santa Cruz, and HeadCount.

For me, I had to stick to my convictions. That was really difficult at times, because I was kind of a lone voice out there.

David Meerman Scott

THE DREAM

"I used to work in the corporate world. I was the Asia marketing director for Knight-Ridder, based in Tokyo and Hong Kong.

I moved to the Boston area in 1995, and was vice president of marketing for NewsEdge Corporation. Thomson acquired them in 2002, and then they sacked me.

That was my opportunity to go out on my own and in 2002 I started a business focused on online marketing consulting.

I started my blog in 2004. In 2007, my book, the *New Rules of Marketing and PR* came out. That has is the top marketing and social media book in the world. "

THE CHALLENGE

The biggest challenge for him was how to convince people that my ideas made sense. As an early content creator, people had trouble understanding the value of using content marketing to drive traffic and conversions for business. Unfortunately, people did not get how the content would drive business, because it did not fit in with conventional wisdom of sales and marketing.

Now, we have clearly proved that educating your clients on how your services can help them is essential to the sales process.

THE ACTIONS

David Meerman Scott's recipe for success

ACTION ONE-HAVE CONVICTION

When you stand alone in your field, you have to have the conviction to believe what you are doing is right.

"If you have an idea that is different than what everyone else thinks, that's often a golden nugget that can be the secret to your success."

ACTION TWO-DREAMS HAPPEN IN INCREMENTS

"What keeps me going is the idea that those opportunities are constantly growing in number and interest. In the very beginning when I started my business, I would wait weeks and weeks and weeks until someone wanted to interview me. I would wait months for someone to ask me to speak at their conference. Each subsequent interview and speech incrementally made me a tiny bit more successful."

The gap between dreams and success happens in many small increments. Each one is important, because it leads to the next step.

ACTION THREE – BUILD YOUR BUSINESS ON INCREMENTAL SUCCESS

"When I started my blog, I didn't have any readers. Not a single reader. I sent a link to the blog to my wife, and then I had one reader. Each incremental success builds upon itself. You build in more success. Again, you have to have those convictions.

You have to say in your head that what I am doing is important, that what I am doing is valuable to people. It is worth doing, and I have to continue to do it. Don't second guess yourself. There were many, many times that I was offered jobs, real jobs, vice president of marketing at well-known companies."

Thankfully, for all of us, David did not take those jobs.

FINAL THOUGHTS

David Meerman Scott's story epitomizes the struggles most people have with keeping up with the times. Many of them are stuck in their old ways. Innovation is a hallmark of success, and something a good entrepreneur always is on the lookout.

➡Here's The Story: Liz Strauss

BIO

Founder of Inside-Out Thinking & SOBCon. Inside-Out Thinking is a high-impact, high-return series of workshops and strategic initiatives customized to each organization.

SOBCon is a unique conference and networking event. First held in May of 2007, it draws the most tightly networked business blogging and social media community on the Internet. SOBCon is a single room, high-intensive focused learning, interactive conversation by the people who make their living on the web.

I get up at about 4:30, and I feel successful by about 10.

It's an every day thing.

Liz Strauss

THE DREAM

"I decided to stay home and do freelance work. I was talking with a friend who worked out in Boston for a company called Delta Education. She said, *Gary, the president of the company, is getting interested in blogs. He is reading the Daily Kos. He knows you. So, if we asked you to write our company, what would you charge?*

I said, I don't know. I'll have to write a blog to find out how much time it takes. That's how I started my writing blog, **Letting Me Be,** in July of 2005. Three months later, I started writing **Successful-Blog.Com.**"

THE CHALLENGE

Liz had some challenges taking on Successful-Blog. The first series that she wrote was hugely popular. However, she ran into some challenges when she announced a second series — on SEO. She asked her programmer to lend expert help, and this was where the problems started for her.

"At that time, Google had just made a major algorithm switch. Liz's programmer was in the UK, which was behind the US at that time. The programmer still supported meta tags, and Google no longer gave them so much weight.

I started this promotion on how we are going to do SEO next. Some of the guys from the Threadwatch, an SEO community came by. They were tough, and regularly skewered each other on Google.

A couple of them, one in particular, came by saying some things in the comment box on that Sunday night. Saying 'you bloggers you don't need SEO. You don't need to know anything about this.'

I said, 'if you think we're going to do this wrong, why don't you hang out to make sure we do it right.' Of course, he didn't do that. He went back to his blog. Monday was a description of the series to come, Tuesday was an overview of SEO that I could handle.

When Wednesday's post by the programmer on metatags came up, the SEO guy wrote his own blog post that sicced his whole community on me. He did it with intent, because linked on the anchor text "here" not to the name of my blog, so I would not get the SEO juice on the backlink.

His whole community started showing up, criticizing me in the comment box.

The next day, Paul Scrivens, who ran the 9 Rules Blog Network, (They were the gold standard of blogging at the time.) supported me. He wrote a blog post in response. The title 'I Don't Know Anything about SEO, but Liz Strauss Is Nice.' was tongue and cheek, because he knows a lot of SEO.

The blog post he wrote was about how the guy who sicced a community on me was basically a jerk. Next thing you know, the guy in question emailed to apologize and gave me a $87 subscription to Aaron Wall's SEO Book as a peace offering.

Meanwhile, in the comment box he got beat up on for about three days. I could name you some people that were in the comment box, and you would know their names. It was very Shakespearean, where the guys put on dresses and play the mean girls parts. It was kind of fun to watch. It was just as catty as any girls' locker room. It was really wild.

THE ACTIONS

Liz's Recipe for success

ACTION ONE-MISTAKES HAPPEN

"If you can't make mistakes online your dead. Don't even bother."

Everyone makes mistakes occasionally. The key is to learn from them. That is why I ask all the speakers, including Liz what their greatest challenge is. Why not learn from their challenges as well as their success, so we can be doubly smart when we encounter both.

ACTION TWO-TAKE CARE OF YOUR CUSTOMER BASE

"I think the most important thing has to do with the relationship with you and your customer base. First, you need to take care of those people who are your core customer base. The ones who will drive 150 miles to see your rock bank playing in a crummy little club. Those guys!

They are the ones who will always stay with you and take care of you. They are really important. They will always see you in a positive light. They will always protect and support you, as opposed to looking for things that are wrong with you. They have your back. I call them the people who won't let you fail.

There was one time I wrote a link post. It was one of those 10-point posts, and every point of the ten had a link in it. I was in a hurry, and the link on the number 8 just had a logical error in the typing, so the link didn't come through.

So, the blog post read, 1,2,3,4,5,6,7...9,10. In the summary under the list, it said it is really important to pay attention to details. Here in this blog post, I obviously did not pay attention to details.

In the first comment in the comment box, it says, 'Whoa! You almost had me with that number 8 there, as if you had done it purpose. It was just 8 blank.' The second person said, 'yeah! you almost had me too.' Me, I am like I blew it."

They were there to make sure, however, that everything was right on the post for future readers.

ACTION THREE-I AM A SOB, & PROUD OF IT

"Friends! I had a lot of, lot of minutes on my phone. There was a time early on, in 2006 that a friend of mine was in sort of a crisis mode. She was living off credit cards after losing her job. She was the primary breadwinner for her family.

As a way to bring her to the attention of my audience, I started something called the Blogger A Day call. I would open up my calendar to anyone who wanted to have an hour with me on the phone. I did that for about 400 days, including weekends.

It was from October, 2006 to all the way to the end of 2007. It was kind of amazing, because by the end of the first week I realized I was going to be basically having the same conversation over and over and over again.

People were so hungry to be heard, and so every day I wrote that I talked to you, and where you lived. First, we discussed his dog, then the cognac he drank, and then the rock band that he plays in. Then I would put a quote at the bottom of it.

Building off the SOB award that became the "bad blogger award" for the blogger a day. It's funny, because there are some pretty big name bloggers that are in there now, but they were pretty small then.

Extreme leadership expert, Steve Farber was a bad blogger. David Armano was a bad blogger. That's how I met them.

You asked me what I did on the bad days, well on the bad days I had all of these people that I could call, because we were all friends. Of course, there wasn't Skype then, or if it was, it was not that good, because we were still using the phone."

I started a reward, and wanted to name it after my blog. Successful Blog was boring, so in the comment area I named it the Successful and Outstanding Blogger Award.

Every week I would give out a SOB award. In response, people would write blog posts where they said, 'Liz called me an SOB and I liked it.' We had a whole directory. Over the course of seven years, there were 385 Saturdays of SOB awards.

So, then when they asked to start the event, they came to me and said we have to bring this party to Chicago. **Chris Cree** actually named the event SOBCon after the SOB award."

FINAL THOUGHTS

I knew that Liz had a cool story, but the twists and the turns of hers are just so cool to hear. This is the reason why I launched *Start Up Gap*. For years, I heard all these amazing things about Liz Strauss. However, we never met. Now that I had the chance to speak with her...she just blew my mind with the cool stuff she was sharing.

➡Here's The Story: Carol Tice

BIO

Carol is the founder of Freelance Writers Den, which currently has over 1200 members. I count myself as a proud member of the den. She is a freelance writer who has written for Forbes, Entrepreneur, American Express, Costco, Dun & Bradstreet, and Yahoo! Jobs among other clients.

I loved the model of mass, where you use the power of mass to drive the price of the content down.

Carol Tice

THE DREAM

"I have been freelancing since 2005. Around 2008, I started a blog, because low rates for freelance writing made me angry.

I discovered a lot of writers unemployed and trying to get into freelance writing. They were getting into content mills, and bid sites. Thinking that $10 per article was a great pay rate. I just really wanted to provide education, enlighten them about better markets that pay better.

That was the start of the *Make A Living Writing* blog. It started on *CarolTice.Com*. As I went along, it became obvious that rants about bad clients was probably not the first things that potential freelance clients want to see.

They were two totally different audiences here. In early 2010, Make A Living Writing was spun out into its own site."

THE CHALLENGE

The biggest challenge to starting the community "was that I knew nothing technically. I had to find people to help me do everything. I could barely run my WordPress blog after somebody else set it up.

I still find things afterwards where I would have to pay people to stick the header on the site. I am very non-technical.

In addition, before 2010 I never sold anything to anyone. I was a reporter. These are new fields. Learning about sales and marketing. I was consuming blogs about sales and marketing constantly.

Reading Social Triggers, DIYThemes, ProBlogger, and CopyBlogger. Just learning about the whole world of selling products online. All new stuff to me."

THE ACTIONS

Carol's Recipe for success:

ACTION ONE-MODEL OF MASS

"I was musing about this idea, 'maybe it would be good if I had a community.' I loved the model of mass, where you use the power of mass to drive the price of the content down, like the Lynda seminars. It is a low monthly rate for all you can eat content.

I loved it in the A-list membership, and I wanted to do it. I know that freelance writers are 'broky' broke. I knew that would be a good model for my audience. I'm like for $25 you can look at 100 hours' worth of stuff. That model worked.

I know a lot of people in this industry are trending towards higher and higher and higher price points. They are selling $1000 things and $3600 things.

The lower I make prices, the more money I make in my space. Don't believe the hype that is all about cooking up some $1000 product. That is not the way it has to go.

ACTION TWO-JUST DO IT!

"I went to SOBCON. I came out of it, and said 'Oh! I should stop musing about it, and launch it in 90 days.' I should just grab a webmaster and create a minimum viable product. Took some old blog posts, and formed some eCourses from them. I set up the forums, and opened the doors.

Then I did a lot of pre-building of the audience for the launch. I did a poll, and then we talked about the results of that poll. What would you want to see in this community? What would you pay?

We had a huge discussion on one blog post about whether there should be an apostrophe in Freelance Writers Den (Note: I double checked; they did not include an apostrophe). Writers care about these things. It was a very impassioned discussion.

At the same time, it was increasing people's awareness, and getting them involved in it.

The other thing I had done to get to 100 members was one on one mentoring. Every time I did that, I said when I open this membership; you are getting a lifetime membership. I gave about 40 people a life time pass, which populated the room initially. They still have that access. That helped.

I offered everyone who took my poll the $17 price versus a $25 when we immediately opened. There was a short time when that was available. We had about 100 people by then.

Then we were open. Then we started creating BUTT LOADS more content to fill it up."

ACTION THREE-GET THE RIGHT TOOLS

These tools made Freelance Writers Den manageable.

"I started with SimplePress, and continue to use this. I know there are better forums now, but I gather we would lose the content we have to switch over. We are going to stay with what we have.

I started Wishlist Member with E-Junkie and PayPal. We found that there were ob-stacles to do everything we wanted to as far as paying affiliates and tracking commis-sions. We had a number of problems with Wishlist.

Then, we switched to Digital Access Pass, which is what we are on now. It is better than Wishlist, but it is still not fully automated. If someone thinks that all the tasks in a membership can be fully automated, you are kidding yourself.

It is semi-automated.

Digital Access Pass (DAP) is signing members up automatically. DAP puts them on the mailing list automatically. Wishlist was not doing that, but we still have to unplug the members.

I have an admin who runs a report twice a week, and unplugs people. That is that part that is not working. I guess the perfect solution is Office Auto-Pilot, which is $500 per month. Not sure if I want to spend $6,000 annually yet.

I learned there is no perfect. You are just wrestling with the technology down to the ground to make it do the things you need to make it do for your business."

FINAL THOUGHTS

Carol's story inspired me so much that when the Freelance Writers Den opened up in April that I joined. Been going through all the amazing information, and I clearly see why she has gone from dreams to success. She has an amazing vision to help freelance writers do more. When we talk about niching down to a target market, or finding some-thing you do that is unique consider what Carol has to say.

➡Here's The Story: Gerald Oginski

BIO

Gerry Oginski has been in practice since 1988. While in law school he worked for a defense medical malpractice insurance company, and began working full time at an aggressive Wall Street law firm handling defense injury and medical malpractice cases. He has owned his own practice, since 2002. In 9 years on *YouTube,* he generated over $8.6 million in settlements for clients.

 The calls triggered that light bulb moment. This is amazing, they are hungry, they are starving for information. That is exactly what I started to do.

Gerry Oginski

THE DREAM

"In 2005, I began to realize that my practice was going downhill. I am a solo practitioner, and one of the amazing things that I was telling you about was that I knew nothing about marketing. I was always getting cases referred to me by other smart attorneys who did not want to handle malpractice cases in New York.

I could not figure out how to generate new cases. I didn't have the budget for TV, big radio campaigns, billboards, or other stuff that other attorneys were doing.

I started learning about a concept called education-based marketing; which really said, 'create a piece of information that teaches your consumers something they want to know about.'

Started to do that with my website by creating blog posts. I kept putting them on my website. It was pretty cool, because it was something very few attorneys were doing at the time.

Then there was this little website that came online in 2006. It had a very funny name, and it said something like now accepting user generated video content. The name of that website was YouTube.

I thought, what the heck is this?

There were a couple of smart marketers, who put attorney TV commercials, because nobody else knew what to do that.

I thought how awful is that? You are not learning anything from an attorney ad. No one is teaching you anything. You have 30 seconds to shout an ad that says come to me, because I am great. Because I have been doing this for 25 years, and you should call me now.

No one ever took the time to answer the question why."

THE CHALLENGE

"The most amazing thing was that I knew nothing about video. Here I am with a 10 year old video camera. I did not know about video, audio, and lighting. I literally had to ask my kids how to turn on my webcam on my Mac computer, because I didn't know how.

The first video looked awful. It was pixelated, dark, and grainy. I had to play with it. I didn't know anything about it. It took me a while to figure out how to create the video, and once I did that, I learned how to put it together and edit it.

I was looking for a way to make it educational, like in the blog posts. I was thinking what I could teach my consumers that they didn't already know yet.

That is very important! People are searching online. You have to understand who is searching for you. That key concept, now you can get into their mind, and say what is going through their minds. What pain do they have? What problems are they experiencing? How can I provide them the answer to some of their pain points.

The first video was "How To Hire A New York Medical Malpractice Lawyer. No one had done that type of content before. That was 6 minutes long. I was so ashamed of where I was shooting my video that I put up a screen behind me, because I didn't want people to know where I was."

THE ACTIONS

Gerald's Recipe for success

ACTION ONE-START LEARNING NOW

"I took that video, and it literally took me a few weeks to figure out how to put it up online and promote it a little bit. I am still an actively practicing trial attorney. I was doing this late at night when my kids went to sleep."

ACTION TWO-CONSISTENCY IS HUGE

"It took me about a year, because in the beginning I thought the equipment was the most important thing. I bought the most expensive video and lighting equipment I could find. The first time I used it was the worst video ever.

Not only did I not know how to get the right settings. It looked beautiful in the camera, but when I uploaded it looked awful. I spent months figuring out what was wrong. I took online courses. The problem was, in 2006, nobody was teaching anybody how to do this.

Took me about a year to learn the process, learn the workflow, which is really important. Once you get the workflow down, you can then focus on the content instead of the actual mechanics.

I create a video every single day now. Every morning, I write at least three articles for my website. Every morning, I edit 2-3 videos, and put them online. I found that being consistent matters in marketing.

Just like an athlete who misses a day, because you are sick or have work. You feel guilty that you have not done that

That is something that I have learned over the past year, and I love it. When you see the correlation between your efforts and the results you get, you will want to do it even more."

ACTION THREE-GIVE PROSPECTS INFORMATION

"My secretary would leave at 2:30 every afternoon. When she left, she would put the phones on service, and all the phone calls would go to my cell phone. I might be in the car on the way to an event, or taking my kids somewhere, and I would get a call.

The call would start out exactly like this.'Mr. Oginski, I just saw your video on this site called *YouTube*. I have some questions, can I ask you something.'

More and more this happened. That taught me people were online actively looking for information about their problem. Whether a medical problem or an injury, now they wanted to learn more about what the lawsuit process was in New York.

It triggered a light bulb moment. This is amazing, they are hungry, and starving for information. That is exactly what I started to do."

FINAL THOUGHTS

"I have over 800,000 views from YouTube. My average views is 15,000 per month. Over the last 8 years, the cases I have taken in from the video marketing have generated in excess of $8.6 million.

What happens is these little online videos educate people.

Chances are they are searching for information, and now they find these videos that are educational that teach them something. Who do you think is much more likely to get a call? Someone who is teaching something new, or someone who has a static website or promotes themselves with come to me without explaining why.

That is why these educational videos work so well. It doesn't have to promote an attorney. Any small business where you want to educate your consumers about things that they don't know."

➡Here's The Story: Yaro Starak

BIO

Entrepreneur, blogger, and cafe writer. I have sold over a million dollars' worth of products via my blogging business.

I focus on helping others start blogs and newsletters based on their passion, and then monetizing the audience they attract by selling digital training products.

I had this sort of holy trinity. It is not religious, but it is very important to me not just for my business, but also for my life.

#1 Time Freedom
#2 Money
#3 Passion

Yaro Starak

THE DREAM

"I started blogging in 2005, and grew my blog over the next two years to the point where I was making a full-time income. Then I started teaching others. This was through a video training course and a lot of affiliate marketing."

While the initial courses he created are not available, he still teaches entrepreneurs how to use blogging for building their business.

THE CHALLENGE

What was interesting to me about Yaro are that his biggest challenges are coming now as he re-formulates his business.

"I am very much reinventing what I am doing online. I am making mistakes, because it is funny when you have a bit of capital you feel a little bit more flexible. Really I should think as if I am broke. I should do this as if I am desperate, which is taking me about a year to get back to doing.

I was making beginning entrepreneur mistakes. I am starting a new business, because I am releasing new training programs, and figuring out my positioning. This is because the market is more crowded today. It is forcing me to do more one on one stuff, and focus on where I need to spend my time."

THE ACTIONS

Yaro's Recipe for success.

ACTION ONE – CREATING SYSTEMS

His first business was a Magic: The Gathering that he started in college, and eventually sold for $13,000. This website kicked off his interest in internet marketing. After college, Yaro started a proofreading business that automated his income.

"We all know what students are like with last minute rush jobs. I was a little tired of checking my email. That was when I had my first taste of outsourcing. I hired a university friend of mine Angela, who is still my virtual assistant today. She has come with us through all the changes.

Back then she took all our email and customer service. That was when I became completely free, and I had about an hour every other day to check in. However, this was when I formulated the holy trinity. Freedom was brilliant, but too much freedom … Money was ok! However, I was not going to make $75,000, let alone $100,000. I covered my bill."

The big thing that was missing was the passion from his business, which is why he started looking for other projects.

ACTION TWO – READING IS CRUCIAL

The freedom and desire to do more lead him to start reading.

"I discovered the 80/20 rule, because I needed justification why I was not working hard. Am I lazy? Am I doing something wrong? The book said, 'no, what you are doing is smart, keep doing it.'

I was reading a particular book at the time on eBay. The Perfect Store told the story of how eBay started. I read this eBay book, and it was amazing, because he started the auction site for his girlfriend to sell her Pez Dispensers.

I came away with one core thing from that book. This thing called the MANY TO MANY MODEL, which is basically a middle man. You have some people buying stuff and some people offering a service or a product. You take a slice of that transaction, and then you can scale on both sites."

Interesting that Carol Tice talked about the many to many model in almost the same exact words. Hmmm! Hmmm!

ACTION THREE – BUILD A CONTENT EMPIRE

"I loved blogging, and I loved writing. I started a podcast in 2005. I wrote an article in 2005 defining podcasting for those who didn't know. It's funny, because it is so big now, but it went through this initial wave, and then it just died.

I finally learned a lesson and added an email newsletter. My list was growing and I had about 3,000 people, which back then was huge.

Then I wasted time. I wrote an eBook over a period of 8 months that never got released, because I was just too slow. I had some mentors who said, 'what are you doing. Get something out of the door.'

Membership sites were becoming popular back then. I said, 'OK! Three months, I am going to do a membership site. It won't be ready, and I would create the membership site with everybody, but I will do a proper launch.' This was back when you had all the original large internet marketing launches.

There was Product Launch Formula with Jeff Walker and Stomper Net with the SEO guys. There was Butterfly Marketing with Mike Filsaine. There was Traffic Secrets from John Reese. I was sort of straddling both worlds between bloggers and internet marketers, and exposed to both ways of making money.

I wanted to do my own launch, and get some affiliates on board. That was when I wrote my first report, The Blog Profits Blueprint (Available on Entrepreneurs Journey)."

FINAL THOUGHTS

Yaro developed a good grasp on how to build the internet systems that he needed for his own life. His philosophy on how he built the business is an inspiration to all internet entrepreneurs, because he understands how to balance the ideas of business and personal growth.

➡Here's The Story: David Oldenburg

BIO

David is the host of the Real Estate Power Show Live airing each Friday at 10am (PT). Topics include Real Estate, Mortgage, Real Estate Current Events, Real Estate Marketing, Social Media, Business, Online Business & Much More!

He is also a mortgage expert: NMLS 235408 and BRE 01131887. 22+ years as a producing loan officer / CEO / branch manager. I do loans in California only. I do FHA, VA, CONV, HARP, JUMBO etc... David helped more than 10,000 people to buy, sell, refinance or invest in real estate.

One of the big things I tell people all the time is find your voice.

David Oldenburg

THE DREAM

"Around 1989 I started to get into the mortgage/real estate industry.

I got started, because my mother was looking to buy a house and I was with her. We were going out and looking at all of these houses and I was meeting realtors she was working with. I remember one day after looking at a couple of houses, I said to her, 'I could do that job. I mean how hard is it to be a realtor?'

My mom called me a couple of days later and said, 'I heard there's this class at this community college. It's a real estate principles class, and if you take the class you can become a realtor.' My mom and I took the class together. We both passed the class.

After the class, I didn't know if I even saw myself doing this as a career. After graduating, I got my certificate, which made me eligible to take the test. I took the California real estate test, passed it, and became a licensed realtor. I didn't really want to do real estate. In other words I didn't want to go sell houses."

THE CHALLENGE

"I'm kind of a numbers guy. I wanted to get into the financial side to become a lender, and you could be a lender with the same license.

I was now legally able to work as a lender but I didn't know anything. I did what anyone else would do. I thought I'm going to walk into a mortgage company and try to get a job.

It didn't go so well. I found a mortgage company I had heard of before, and I walked in the door dressed really nice and asked for the broker of record. This lady comes out looks like a Nordstrom woman. She was dressed really nice. She said, "Sure, I'll talk to you about coming to work for the company."

We go back to her office and she asks me a bunch of questions trying to find out whether I'd be good at sales, I had a following, or been in the mortgage industry for any length of time.

After about 30 minutes of talking to me she said, 'Dave, you seem like a nice guy, but I have no interest in hiring you. You have no following, and you have no experience. You're just not a good fit for us.' Basically thanks, but no thanks.

I walked out very discouraged. I thought, gosh, it's going to be a lot harder to get a job in this industry than I thought. I went home, and I didn't think I did anything for a week. I went back to my job and kind of forgot about the real estate and mortgage industry."

THE ACTIONS

Dave's recipe for success

ACTION ONE-START AT STEP ONE, NOT STEP TEN

"I think it was about a week later, and I was looking at the help wanted ads in the Sacramento Bee under real estate and finance. I came across an ad that said Loan Officers Wanted. No experience necessary. We will train. I thought this is my job. I called the phone number, made an appointment, and went out and met the guy, who was like a used car salesman. It was a total boiler room operation. Everybody is on the phone. Everybody is making deals.

I go to work for this company, and sure enough they give me training. You know what my training was? 'Hey Dave, here's a bunch of business cards, go out and get a bunch of business.' So I'm working at this company. It's a boiler room operation. I don't want to say it was a sleazy operation, but it definitely was on the border.

This is where I got really good on the phone, and for that I'm thankful. They would run these advertisements, and back then it wasn't as regulated as it is today. You didn't have the Federal Truth in Lending. Back then they used to run radio ads something like — Get a 30-year mortgage with a rate of 3%. Back then rates were 7%, so if you heard on the radio that you could get a 30 year mortgage with a rate of 3%, you're going to pick up the phone and call.

For two years, I sat around 40-50 hours a week on the phone talking to people and making sales. That was a blessing in disguise, because the company wasn't great. However, it taught me a skill that I went on to use and make a lot of money with later on. It got me really confident on the phone."

ACTION TWO-MARKETING AND SALES ARE HUGE

"It's 1992 and I'm a top producer in the mortgage industry. I'm making good money, doing 20-30 deals a month by myself with no extra assistance, staff, or anything. Keep in mind it was easier to do loans in the 90s. You didn't have all the paperwork you have today.

Let me fill in the gap here, because I went from working for someone to being in business for myself. What happened in the interim is that I went to work for two mortgage companies and they ended up going bankrupt.

I saw all the mistakes they made. They treated their employees poorly, did things that were unethical, had terrible commission splits, and just weren't professionally run companies. I did what a lot of people do. I said I could run a company so much better than these people do, if only I went out there and ran my own company.

As far as building the clientele, I did this through the radio show and blogging. I was blogging way back in 1995 before most people were blogging. I was building my e-mail lists. At the end of my radio show, I'd give people my website which was called — Your Money.

People would go to my website, and back in 1995 there was no video. A website was primarily text only, and every once in awhile you'd have a little image. There were no contact forms; nothing. When people came to my website, they'd see a little picture of me, some text talking about my show and what I did. I had my email address in there and said — hey, if you'd like to hear from me each week, if you'd like to find out what I'm doing, learn more about my guests, and about the real estate industry, copy and paste this e-mail address into your e-mail account and send me an e-mail.

Through blogging, e-mails, and hosting shows I was able to build a good referral base of people that referred me business and allowed me to go to that next level in the mortgage industry, which ultimately led to making millions of dollars doing that.

I get more referrals and more business and network with more people and have more success using my phone. More than social media, more than my radio show, more than any other form of communication. I think one of the problems is that people are afraid to pick up the phone, and simply call people and engage. You have to get over that fear. If you want to know people, you have to pick up the phone.

I worked for a Wall Street boiler room type company and I got real good at using the phone. So for me picking up the phone and cold calling somebody and saying — 'Hey, I'd like to introduce myself. My name is David Oldenburg, etc., etc.' I can do that very easily."

ACTION THREE – BUILDING A SCALABLE BUSINESS

"I had been successful before, so I had put away some money. I had the resources to put together $100,000. I had a guy come on as a partner, and he put in $25,000 of his own money. So I had to come up with $75,000 of my own money. I had to get out there and get everything organized and I did.

We took that company from not existing to being a fully functioning mortgage company doing business with the public in about 30 days. It was insane. I was working 24 hours a day.

Over six years I built that from nothing to a company with 50 employees and multi-seven figure revenue, became a major mortgage player in my area, and grew by leaps and bounds. There was a lot that transpired from starting that company in 30 days to getting to that point.

For example, I'm six months into the business. I have ten people working for me, I have a full time loan processor, and we're starting to do deals. My overhead was low, because I had bought everything up front. I only had to meet payroll.

That was great, but I had one problem. I wanted to recruit. I wanted to get bigger, I wanted to market. This is where I launched the radio show. For those of you sitting out there that own a business, and are trying to promote it, radio is just a platform just like a Google Hangouts, blog, and website.

People will watch me sometimes and they'll say, "Dave that's awesome for you but it's not me." It doesn't matter though. Take what I said, and apply it to a platform that works for you.

I chose radio. I wanted to be able to promote my business and recruit. This could be a completely new conversation.

I got a radio show, and used that show to become more influential. I brought people I wanted to become closer with onto the show as guests. I had people calling into the show asking questions about real estate, finance and other things.

I used that radio show to springboard the business, to meet more people, to build credibility and you can do that with a blog or a website. You can do it passing out your business card at a chamber of commerce meeting. My platform was radio, but you can choose whatever you're good at.

It let me build more credibility in my industry and people were like — I know that guy. What ended up happening is that when people lost their jobs or wanted to go to work for a different mortgage company people would end up calling me, because they knew me. They'd say — hey Dave, I heard you before. I want to come work for you. That was how I recruited a lot of people in to work for me."

FINAL THOUGHTS

David's story is fascinating. First, I thought it was interesting that he struggled when he first started in the industry, because he had to learn a completely new set of skills after being a paramedic. Second, while he is smooth on live shows now, it took a lot of practice.

➡️Here's The Story: Jeff Bullas

BIO

Jeff is a social media marketing blogger, keynote speaker, digital strategist, consultant, and best-selling author. He works with companies to optimize their online personal and company brand through social media channels and other web technologies.

His blog, JeffBullas.Com, is about all things to do with social media, content and digital marketing.

This is not a destination. This is a journey. Don't think you're going to turn up in some Nirvana one day saying — Hallelujah, I have arrived! That's not what it's about.

Jeff Bullas

THE DREAM

"I was initially trained as a teacher and got involved in the technology industry fairly early on, so I didn't teach for very long. I moved into the technology and telecommunications industry and then into the web."

I was basically unemployed and had a lot of time. I was reading a lot of books and I was inspired by a few elements. One was I got on Facebook and noticed people's obsession with Facebook. Then I got on Twitter, and didn't really know what to do with Twitter.

Like a lot of people have discovered as they got on, I wondered what's this 140 characters about?

Then I was really inspired by 3 key elements — Tim Ferriss' 4 Hour Work Week, David Meerman Scott's New Rules of Marketing and PR, and the third inspiration in terms of external motivation was a blog by Hubspot. They said if you have an inkling of something that you're interested in or would like to start a blog on, just start. Don't think too much about it. Those were my three external motivators.

On top of that, I reached a point in my life where I thought what if I reached 80 or 90? What dent have I made in the universe? So it was a bit of what legacy would I leave if I was looking back in life? I said, 'Well not really much. Not much of a digital footprint.'

So I just had an inkling, I spent $10 on a domain and I started in March, 2009."

THE CHALLENGE

"I suppose the technology. Where do I start? Like how do I even Tweet? It really was a challenge. I had to overcome a lot of fears I suppose that were not really big fears, but when you add up ten little fears they sort of become a bigger fear.

Just starting is one of the most powerful things that you can do. I posted something the other day on my Facebook page and on Google+, which was that done is better than perfect. That is something that really resonates with me, because if you wait to be perfect you'll never do anything."

THE ACTIONS
Jeff's recipe for success

ACTION ONE-HAVE A GO TO SOCIAL NETWORK

"I'm really an accidental blogger. I never started off with any grand plan. I didn't say I was going to get rich. I didn't say that I was going to get millions of followers and I'm going to be doing what I'm doing today.

It was just a combination of passion, some ability coupled with a lot of curiosity, and some experience in the technology and web world.

So how did I do it? Twitter has really been my online weapon of choice. I started following people on Twitter, and followed almost everyone that had a bit of a following or a heartbeat.

My plan on Twitter was very uncoordinated and random. Then I started getting smarter, as I made more mistakes and learned from those. Then people seemed to enjoy what I was writing. I got picked up, and put on a couple of lists such as Social Media Examiner and a couple of others, such as *Forbes* and *Huffington Post*.

Being discovered and put on a list caused people to start turning up and in bigger quantities."

ACTION TWO-FIND SOMETHING YOU ARE GOOD AT AND LIKE

"I think the real power to creating and marketing a blog that matters is starting from the right foundation.

This is sometimes really hard to discover. You have to have a passion, and the passion could be a mix of things. It could be technology, writing, marketing and curiosity. That's a synthesis of some of the passions that I have.

I think on top of that you need to couple that with your abilities and experience. It's actually passion coupled with experience and also that plugs into innate abilities.

It sounds easy and sometimes it is. Some people know what they want to do from when they were 3 years old. Other people never discover it and go to their graves with their song unsung and that's really sad. I think this is a journey people need to explore with friends and family.

Quite often I think what's important, and this is what excites me about the social web, is the art of creating and expressing. You almost plug in to what I call, and this almost sounds new age, the super conscious of the planet and get feedback in real time.

And that's a real guidance in terms of what you should be doing. When you're on social media you start connecting with your tribe. That's important, because sometimes friends and family are your biggest enemies. They're say you're crazy, you're stupid, and maybe don't appreciate the magic you have within you.

I think you have to start with the synthesis of the key elements and as I said, it's no singularity. It's actually a matrix of synergy."

ACTION THREE – BUILD YOUR LIST

"I didn't get into list building until about a year afterwards, and I didn't do as well with it as I should have.

Giveaway something free — free video, free eBook. It doesn't have to be a big eBook, 10 or 15 pages. Just do something to build that list from day one.

Number two has been Twitter for me. I have automated it and that saves me about 100 hours a month. It also keeps my content in front of people in the Twitter stream.

I relentlessly built my list. I don't actively do it too much now because it grows organically. I do it through Twitter like strategies.

I use a couple of tools — Twellow, Tweepi, Social Oomph, & Twitter feed to help me consistently create great content as well"

FINAL THOUGHTS

An "accidental blogger!" Jeff created one of the coolest blogs on the internet by accident. That sort of baffles me, because as an avid reader of his blog for the past 3 years I can tell you his content is meticulously developed. The ideas are fresh and unique!

Side note: as an occasional blogger on his site, the content somehow gets better on those days. That notion aside, I always thought Jeff's blog is one of the best resources for social media on the web full of great tutorials.

➡Here's The Story: Steve Olsher

BIO

New York Times Bestselling Author, International Keynote Speaker, and host for *Internet Prophets: The World's Leading Experts Reveal How to Profit Online.*

> So I think the *Start Up Gap* was trying to figure out what the hell am I doing here? The *Start Up Gap* really boils down to clarity.
>
> *Steve Olsher*

THE DREAM

"In author land, they say you write the book that you most need. I'm still trying to figure that out. I think it sometimes varies by the day, but it's a work in progress. My gifts lie in communication, and so that's kind of the overarching theme that ties everything together.

About five years ago, I got more into the personal development side of the work. I had a moment of truth, or epiphany if you will. I was by my stepfather's side. He was literally in his final days of life, and he couldn't talk anymore, but I think we were able to communicate through touch.

I had a vision of my funeral. I could hear the words being spoken graveside. They were — Here lies Steve Olsher. He dedicated his life to chasing the almighty dollar. And that was all that was said. It hit me hard, because it was clear that up to that point my life only had meaning to those closest to me and myself, but no one else.

I had this nagging and tugging at my collar that I was meant and made to do something extraordinary. That's really kind of what moved me down the path to put pen to paper. That was the first step into this arena to write and to share some of the tips, tools, strategies and shortcuts that have been helpful to me in the hope of potentially helping others."

THE CHALLENGE

"Ramping up, because we live in this instant gratification world of wanting everything now and it's a process. I think that's the hardest part. I'm someone who operated at warp speed for my entire career.

I don't have a million followers like Gary Vaynerchuk. I don't have 4 million people in my circles like Guy Kawasaki. I'm certainly no Tony Robbins by any stretch. I think I've made a nice little dent in the time that I have been doing this, and I have a long way to go.

I think that's the hardest part. Just recognizing that it's a transition."

THE ACTIONS

Here's how Steve found success.

ACTION ONE-THE PROCESS, THE BEACON

"I literally just wrote a blog post on this yesterday. The title was Hope is a Mother F*ck@r. That's the reality. I think that as authors, entrepreneurs, and agents of change, we get this "thing" embedded in us. I don't know what it is.

Think of someone like Nelson Mandela who endured ungodly treatment for years. Yet he had a beacon of light, that hope he somehow received inside him. He had to stay the course, because he knew that at some point he was going to be in a position to really uplift his fellow countrymen.

But why him? Why Nelson Mandela? Why does he end up with that beacon? That's kind of what I struggle with. Where does this beacon come from?

It's really a long answer to your question. I think embedded within each of us is perhaps what you'd call your mission. Some people will call it your destiny, some people will call it their reason for being. This beacon is kind of like your friend's 3-year old. You can try to ignore it, but you're not going to shut it up. That's just the reality. That's what keeps me motivated. It isn't anything external. It's built in the DNA and there isn't anything."

ACTION TWO-FIND JOINT VENTURE PARTNERS

"The most powerful way to get your message out, to get traffic, etc., is to find joint venture partners. Find people who are in yours or similar spaces, who will introduce you to their audiences.

Even though I was online since 1993, a lot of people didn't know who I was. The more I got into the personal development space and the more into the internet marketing space certain names kept coming up. I figured I had to get on their radar, and the only way to get on their radar was to add value for them. That's where the concept for Internet Prophets came.

I came up with the title, bought the domain, and thought this would be a great opportunity for me to try to connect with some of these folks. So that's where I started entrenching myself into the industry by connecting with Mike Filsaime, Armand Morin, Steve Harrison, Mike Ostrovsky, and on and on. Lots of really great folks who have done amazing things.

I basically did the same thing that you're doing, which is saying give me an hour of your time. I'll interview you, transcribe this whole thing, rewrite chapters, etc. The book is based on these interviews with these 25 people.

Once they saw the product I created they were like –wow, this guy is legit. What he created is good. Then the book started getting awards, and that put me on the proverbial map. Then that provided me the ability to partner with some of them to get the word out about what I was doing."

ACTION THREE-GET IT DONE!

"I think my greatest habit is also my greatest curse. My greatest habit is that I really move to get it done, but I do so in a way that only I can do. That's not a great place to be.

My habit is that once I get an idea I usually ram it down the throats of whomever it needs to go through until it comes to fruition. It's cool that it gets done, but I just don't trust anyone. If I've got the right idea and I think it's going to work, come hell or high water it's going to get done. But it doesn't mean that I'm willing to turn over the reins along the way."

While I am not advocating Steve doing things that only you could do, because that negates any system you could create. He definitely hustles for what he wants. That ability to be confident and go for your dreams is an essential Gapper trait.

FINAL THOUGHTS

Steve really said it best on the development of his story.

"It's taken me every bit of 5 years to truly understand the framework for what I created. It really boils down to this, using your gifts and the vehicle you use to share those gifts with the world and people you're most compelled to serve.

The gifts, the vehicle, and the people are the three crucial elements. It's taken me every bit of 5 years to figure that out through a lot of trial and error. So I think the *Start Up Gap* was trying to figure out what the hell am I doing here? Now I've got something that's reflective of the culmination of this work. The *Start Up Gap* in my opinion boils down to clarity."

➤Here's The Story: Anita Campbell

BIO

Founder of Small Business Trends, the most popular, independent small-business blog and community on the Web. We help readers stay on top of trends in small business.

Also owner of BizSugar.com, the premier social media and bookmarking site specifically for small businesses.

 You have to think of it like walking upstairs. You take a step and grow a little bit and that helps you bring in a little bit of revenue and that funds you to go to the next step.

Anita Campbell

THE DREAM

"I never started out to be an internet entrepreneur. I started my career as a lawyer, and spent most of it in-house working for companies and enjoyed it. I liked it a lot, but in the 1990s I wanted to do something different. So, at Bell & Howell, where I worked at the time, I got involved in e-commerce. I started an internal start up, an intra-preneurial start up, if you will. Grew that and then I left Bell & Howell in the early 2000s and wasn't sure what I wanted to do.

I started consulting for some friends of mine who wanted business plans. They just wanted help with their start-ups, and before I knew it I thought, you know, I'm actually a consultant. Maybe I'll put up a consulting website and maybe I ought to market this consulting business.

Then I started an e-mail newsletter. I wanted to use the e-mail newsletter to market the business and I needed a way to publish some articles. A friend of mine said why don't you u Blogger.com, and start one of those blog things. This was in 2003. I had heard of blogs, but didn't know what they were.

I tried Blogger and was blown away with how easy it was. It was so easy to publish compared to anything else before. I was playing around with Dreamweaver trying to publish articles. I wasn't very good at Dreamweaver. It was a nightmare. It was taking me 2 days to get articles published for a newsletter, and I thought I can't do this. I'll be spending all of my time on newsletters and marketing. Blogger changed everything.

Fast-forward about 6 months. I had many more readers on the blog than I did on the e-mail newsletter, and the rest is history. I decided to focus on the site itself. From there the blog became the business. It actually took over and I stopped consulting eventually. Now I'm a publisher."

This was the start of her blog Small Business Trends. Skipping forward to 2009, she purchased BizSugar.

"What happened was that I knew the former owner of BizSugar, and at Small Business Trends we would share our content on BizSugar. We had a couple of phone calls, and one thing led to another and I said you know, 'what if I were to buy BizSugar from you?'

THE CHALLENGE

"The biggest challenge overall is finding enough money to invest to grow. As a start-up entrepreneur, you have to remember that you must invest to grow. You might think you can get by with never spending any money, but the reality is you have to spend sometimes. You can have limited money, but you have to figure out where to spend it.

You have to have a long-term view also, because money is always limited. You never have as much as you'd like.

You have to think of it like walking upstairs. You take a step, you grow a little bit, that helps you bring in a little bit of revenue, and that funds your next step.

Then you grow a little bit more, you get a little more revenue in, you can invest it back into the business and you keep walking up steps. That's what the whole process is like. Finding the money to get started so it doesn't take you forever — that's always the challenge."

THE ACTIONS

Here's how Anita found success.

ACTION ONE – NETWORKING IS HUGE

"One of the things we did early on, just through making networking connections, was make a connection with American Express Open. Even back in 2005 they were actually paying me as a blogger to attend events, write about them, and share those events with our audience (all disclosed, of course). Now this is before the days of Twitter. Blogs were the social media at the time and that was very forward thinking of them.

I made a connection with a PR person who was living in the Netherlands. She found me online, and we ended up just emailing and eventually talking by phone. What it really proves to me is that you must be open to connect, especially through email. So many internet entrepreneurs, for reasons I don't understand, are kind of hostile toward answering emails. They don't want to be bothered.

You don't know at first what something is going to lead to. You don't know, and I will tell you that 98% of the emails are just going to take up your time. They aren't going to necessarily lead to anything, but you know that 2% will. It's how you put yourself out. We're having this conversation, and maybe this doesn't lead to anything directly. However, indirectly it could lead to something huge for you or for me. You have to be open to that.

That's one thing I would encourage people to do — make yourself accessible. I know it takes a lot of time, but try to be as accessible as possible. It can really pay off.

American Express was a yearlong sponsor for BizSugar and that really helped us because when you get that money coming in and you can count on it, you can use that money to invest.

ACTION TWO-MANAGE YOUR SENSE OF OPTIMISM

"I think a lot of it is managing your sense of optimism. I really believe that because on any given day, and I'm sure you run into this as well Andy, there are a hundred things that can go wrong and probably do go wrong.

If you let yourself get depressed, because this didn't go right or that wasn't right or someone didn't like this or that, or my website got hacked or whatever — you really have to take an attitude that says hey, whatever comes I'm going to handle it. Whatever is thrown at me I'm going to deal with it.

I always try to measure the progress we've made. I'm really big on numbers and I even have reports sent to myself. I have Google Analytics reports emailed to me. I have various social media reports emailed to me. I have various membership reports sent to me and moderator stats sent to me.

All of those things — and it's not like I'm a numbers geek or anything — it's because when I can see a little progress, but it really pumps me up and I need that. Even if it's a small little thing I have to have it. I have to see some progress.

Even if it's like ten extra followers on Twitter. You set little goals for yourself. We got ten new followers this week; let's see if we can get twenty next week."

One of the things that we did that helped us grow was, if you're familiar with re-targeting, retargeting ads. There was a new start-up at the time called Retargeter.com. They had this concept of retargeting ads. I thought for BizSugar that could really work because what we want to do is keep reminding members or people who have visited the site to come back and keep sharing their content.

Now it doesn't work for every situation, but for BizSugar it was really ideal. I think this was one key tactic that helped us grow. For a couple of years we ran a monthly re-targeting ad campaign. If you had visited BizSugar and you went to another site that was running these retargeted ads, you would see ads for BizSugar. You could go to CNN.com for example, and see a BizSugar ad on it. Of course, we could never have afforded to advertise directly on CNN.com and other sites like that. Many big media sites were similar.

Through retargeting, because we were targeting the people who had visited before, and we wanted to remind them, create that sense of loyalty, and stay top of mind, it worked really well.

It was cost effective, because we were paying about $500 a month at the time and we got a limited number of retargeted impressions, but it was enough to help build that up."

ACTION THREE-ATTENTION TO DETAIL

"I think there are two things. One of them is a lot of attention to detail. I think you have to be a sort of big picture thinker and long-term thinker but you have to have the ability to deal with the details. The devil is in the details in all of this stuff. That actually took me a long time to learn. People say I'm really detail oriented, but for a long time I was all about ideas, big ideas. Nothing ever got done.

It wasn't until I forced myself to write things down a lot. I write detailed things, like plans, reports, and outlines. I find that really helps, otherwise the ideas just sort of disappear. Just writing it down forces you to think it through in detail. It helps you communicate with your team or outside stakeholders. It just helps things take shape I find. That's one thing.

Another thing is just this capacity to deal with problems. Now that's something I've always been good at. I compartmentalize. Sometimes I have to say I'm not going to worry about this right now. I'll put it on my calendar and I'll worry about it tomorrow. It really helps. There's actually science behind it.

If you're familiar with David Allen — Getting Things Done — great book and great mechanism for time management. I read something that said there's science behind it, and the science is your brain energy gets frittered away if you have too many things you have to think about. If you can think about one or two things, you have more energy to solve the problem.

You have to clear your brain out — — that's what the compartmentalizing does. You can focus on one problem better than worrying about sixteen problems. You write stuff down, put it on a calendar, just get it out of your head and focus on that one thing."

FINAL THOUGHTS

"I think there's a long way to go yet, so I wouldn't beat my chest and say I'm so successful. I'm always looking at what more we can do. In my case, because everything we've done is self-funded it's taken longer. It's been slower.

I would say we had an extended start-up period but I don't mind that at all because I've been able to sleep at night. I haven't had to worry about my house being foreclosed on or whatever. I know there are business owners and entrepreneurs that do have that concern, but maybe they grow faster. Maybe they take that risk and they grow faster. I just felt that I wanted it a little bit slower. I wish it wasn't quite as slow. I wish things were a lot faster always but that's the choice I made."

➡ Here's The Story: Chef Dennis Littley

BIO

My name is Dennis Littley or "Chef Dennis" as I'm known both at work and across the blogsphere, I am an Executive Chef, Culinary Instructor, Recipe Developer and most recently an Award Winning Food Blogger and Photographer.

I am now enjoying semi-retirement in Florida.

I began blogging in 2009 as a resource for my culinary students, and soon found myself with followers around the world, at which time I began posting *"real food recipes for real people."*

 Things are going to happen. It's how you react to how things happen.

Chef Dennis Littley

THE DREAM

"I started in the food industry when I was 12 flipping burgers in fast food joints.

In the 1980's, I started working white tablecloth restaurants, and went through an apprenticeship. I worked my way through a series of different jobs.

The last job I had was at a school and that was how I started this adventure that I'm on now. I started a cooking program at the school, and I'd have times when I couldn't print out the recipes. I said let me start a blog. I'll put the recipes there and people can come pick them up and it'll be easier.

None of my students ever went to the blog, but all of the sudden I had readers from all over the world.

I started my blog in November of 2009. It was ugly as sin. I don't think my first post had images. Once I started adding them, they weren't much better.

If I knew then what I know now to be successful as a blogger I'd have run screaming from the room and found something else to do. But a $5,000 camera later and numerous blog designs — we're still at it with *AskChefDennis.com*."

THE CHALLENGE

"It was getting over being afraid of being in front of the camera, and all of the glitches that we have when we do hangouts. Just like yesterday it was down and I lost two shows. It's facing them, understanding there's not a whole lot you can do about it, taking a deep breath and just moving on.

I think that's the biggest problem most people have. They expect perfection. It's not going to happen. This is live TV. Things happen, and you have to embrace it, do not get so upset about it.

I think the turning point for me with that was I taught a lot of classes in a lot of bad situations where people in their kitchens didn't have very good setups. People decided they were going to take the class on iPads when iPads weren't supported well. They would go in and out. I finished one class on the telephone. You just have to figure out a way.

The first thing I ever did for Google — Google e-mailed me and wanted to talk to me. I was like, 'oh my God, Google wants to talk to me.'

They wanted me to do a Thanksgiving promo for them and I was one of four people in the country that was doing this. I was so excited and I worked out this whole big thing and halfway through it my microphone goes.

I hear the people in the peanut gallery going — Chef, we can't hear you. Therefore, I had to walk over and change my microphone. My headset wasn't working, so I had to change that. I just continued and I talked to Google. They were like you handled that really well. I was relieved. They said, "That's ok. Things happen. We like to see how you handle it. You handled it really well." They were fine.

That was an ah-ha moment. They didn't expect it to be perfect. Things happen. It's how you react to how things happen."

THE ACTIONS

The Chef's recipe for success.

ACTION ONE-HAVE A PLATFORM TO DISCUSS YOUR BUSINESS

"Most of the changes came with the start of Google+. I had my blog and I think every blogger has these aspirations of being the next Pioneer Woman setting the world on fire and making millions of dollars. The truth was for the longest time my brother and his wife were the only ones reading my blog. Then it started to develop.

I never expected it to get that much. I just wanted to make enough extra money to supplement my retirement plan. It wasn't costing me any money.

By doing that, I positioned myself to be picked up by the first hangout classes that were on Google+.

It was ChefHangout.com. This was at a time when no one was using hangouts for what they were intended for, so Google embraced us. They verified most of our team and me at a time when only celebrities were being verified. They pushed me out on a follow list for a month, which really helped. Most of the team was on for a year, but I only got on for a month so I had to work harder.

I think that's what did it. The fact that I had to work for what I was getting made it more valuable to me. Not that the people that were on the list didn't deserve what they got, I'm not saying that. Anytime you have to knuckle down and bust your butt to do something the rewards are sweeter.

Google has really been the mainstay for me now and the hangouts and my shows."

ACTION TWO-FIND A WAY TO PURSUE YOUR PASSION

"I'm happy when I'm feeding people. That's probably my biggest joy. My second biggest joy is introducing my friends to each other.

I had to step out of cooking this year with a series of injuries. I just couldn't be in the kitchen for ten hours a day anymore. I had to step back. When I stepped back, the social media aspect of Google became what I really focused on. It became my replacement for being in the kitchen.

One of my Google+ friends was kind of smacking me in the face saying well your name is Chef Dennis, it's not Marketer Dennis or SEO Dennis, so you better get your ass back in the kitchen and start cooking. It was an ah-ha moment. I was like alright, I belong in the kitchen.

I always told my wife when she asked what do you want to get out of this when I started this whole thing — well, I'd like to be a household name and I'd like to be on The Ellen Show. Those are my two goals.

I wasn't looking to make all the money in the world. Money is always a by-product of what you do that makes you happy and I'm happy doing what I'm doing now. I think I'm also positioning myself to make some money, but you know if it doesn't happen, I'm not going to worry all day about it and not be able to sleep. But if it does happen I'll just be traveling more."

ACTION THREE – READ AND RESEARCH OTHERS THOUGHTS

"The fact that I can read and I'm not afraid to research something is probably my greatest tool. I've learned a lot from people. I take ideas and I never use something exactly as I see it. I refine it. I'll make it my own. You know you can't reinvent the wheel every day. It's impossible but you can make it yours.

You know I'll look at a recipe. I won't read it, but I'll see what it is and I'll go and make it the way I want it."

FINAL THOUGHTS

Chef Dennis is almost giddy talking about what he does. You can feel the passion seeping out of what he does. Plus, I will have to admit that I now want to take a road trip to Florida to have a dinner that he made. Just looking at all the delicious meals he shows on Google+ makes me hungry.

➡️Here's The Story: Tom Heskin

BIO

Throughout my fifty plus years of experience in the electrical industry, I have developed an extensive background in both lighting design and value engineering practices which enables us to offer additional savings to our customers.

In 2010, we realized we could offer our existing & new customers heating-cooling services as well and it was a win-win situation all around. We offer year round maintenance of existing heating-cooling systems for all types of systems.

The greatest habit is striving for customer satisfaction based on the fact that if you have a happy customer they'll tell 10 people and if you have an unhappy customer they'll tell 100 people.

Tom Heskin

THE DREAM

"My father was a contractor. He started the business back in 1956. My father started me out in kindergarten, fifty cents for a half day, a dollar for the whole day.

I was putting plates on outlets throughout the home. They were mainly crooked and had to be straightened afterwards. I went from a young kid to the shop boy to the driver to the runner to the helper on the job site, learned the trades, and went away to college. Eventually came back to work with my dad.

He later retired and I bought the business and expanded it from there." Tom bought the business in 1986.

THE CHALLENGE

"I'd say the biggest change was back in 2001. Got out of new construction and went strictly into services, which was a 180 degree about face. It was a great decision, because when we had the building crash back in '07 and '08 unfortunately a lot of other contractors weren't able to weather the storm.

At that point, people weren't selling their homes and buying bigger. They were fixing up what they had and we went into people's homes and modifying existing systems. Around that same time is when we decided to add the heating and cooling and started repairing heating and cooling systems as well."

THE ACTIONS

Tom's Recipe for success

ACTION ONE-ADAPT TO THE MARKET

"Having the vision to see the other markets out there. In the service industry, it's more of an on demand need in lieu of a project that's being planned months in advance.

In the service arena people call you with immediate needs, and you have to be able to react on an immediate basis. Sometimes you have some leeway or a window.

For instance, today I was up in Kenosha, Wisconsin for a gentleman that was concerned about the basement flooding in the near future, because he's right on Lake Michigan. That's a case that's not an immediate need. You get a set of blueprints and you have to bid on it."

ACTION TWO-STAY AT THE FOREFRONT OF TECHNOLOGY

"The technology in our industry keeps advancing. Last month I took a class on the full home dimming systems, because now you can control your entire home's electrical system from your smartphone. Tomorrow I'm taking a class in motorized drapes that'll integrate with the same system.

Twenty years ago, the standby generator was hooked up to a manual transfer switch that the generator would run, but someone would have to flip the power from Commonwealth Edison over to the generator. Now that's all automated.

The same thing with the heating and cooling systems. The furnaces are getting smaller, they're computerized and they talk to your cell phone if there's a problem with them. I think my interest in the industry stays active, because of the fact that the technology keeps changing. We have to stay on top just to keep offering the latest and greatest to our customers."

ACTION THREE-CUSTOMERS COME FIRST

"I think the greatest habit is striving for customer satisfaction based on the fact that if you have a happy customer they'll tell 10 people and if you have an unhappy customer they'll tell 100 people. I think that in today's economy you have to strive for customer satisfaction. That's got to be your main goal.

Another key is staying in contact with them. We give our customers windows meaning between and 8 and 12 or 1 and 5. You never know what the duration would be of the call that the technician is on before he gets to the next customer. The customer that's waiting their arrival could often be antsy.

It's imperative that our office calls the customer a couple of times giving them a heads up letting them know when our arrival time will be, so they're not left in the dark waiting."

FINAL THOUGHTS

Tom is a model of continuity. He just keeps making sure his company is better. One of the interesting things interviewing him is he focuses on the core of his business: customers. Find out what they want, and deliver it.

➡ Here's The Story: Andy Nathan

Yes I did! I interviewed myself for April Fools day. However, the content was awesome (no bias), and I decided to include it.

BIO

Andy Nathan is the founder of Smart at the Start, a blog and social networking consulting company that helps small businesses grow through bite-sized internet marketing services. He successfully worked with hundreds of entrepreneurs in over 75 different industries over the past four years.

I look back at things I did two years ago and how it makes a difference now. That's really cool when you think about it.

Andy Nathan

THE DREAM

"I was 25, and had been a teacher for three years. It just wasn't the right fit for me. I knew I wanted to do something else with my life, and started looking around for other options. This got me into mortgages through a series of classes, connections, and networking.

Something happened at my first mortgage job that got me started down the path of entrepreneurship. One of the loan officers mentioned something that was profound to me.

He said, 'If you buy ten properties now and pay them all off by the time you retire, you will never have to worry about what you do once you retire.'

That idea was kind of mind blowing to me at the time.

What he was talking about was that if I spent the next 10–15 years paying off one property, and put all my time and energy into that one property, I could have a free and clear rental property. Then I can buy a second property and then a third property and then a fourth property and so on. By the time, I retired in 40 years he said you'd have everything you needed.

However, 30 to 40 years seemed like way too much time for so little reward. Therefore, I started looking into how to build a business. I looked into real estate, and I bought a property in Schaumburg. I rented out the second bedroom, and I lived in the first bedroom.

What happened was, a few years down the road, I said this is nice, but let's pick this up some more. I want to do more with this. This isn't happening fast enough, so I bought a property in Arlington Heights with my dad. Then I bought a property in Florida and eight more properties in Indiana. It was nice, saying 'you're a property owner' and you have all of these properties, but I bought right around the time — 2008–2009 — a lot of bad stuff happened in the economy. Unfortunately, because of those changes I lost or sold all of those properties.

I finally reached a point where I knew I made a mistake. I knew I needed to have a way to support myself and the real estate and mortgage business wasn't working anymore. Subsequently, I started looking around for what I could do."

THE CHALLENGE

"My biggest challenge was when I had all of those problems with the properties. It did something mentally to me. I didn't know how to get free from it. It's like the weight of the world is on your shoulders.

My wife and I got married in 2009, and it wasn't a good time financially. I'm forever grateful she stayed married to me, because it was a tough transition. I switched careers, married, and moved all within two months. Talk about stressful living. I had to catch up with my brain. Once I did that, I was able to form my current business.

It took me seven months to get into social media, but I took a lot of lessons from real estate. Part of the problem with real estate was that I wasn't really focused. Every week I was doing a new thing trying to figure out what I should do."

THE ACTIONS
My recipe for success

ACTION ONE-FOCUS ANDY-SAN!

"With internet marketing, I was more focused. No, jumping from venture to venture. People would ask me to do other things and I was like No, No, No. I didn't partner with people the first year after real estate, because I didn't want to lose my focus. I was afraid of losing that focus. I just wanted to go my own route. Eventually that changed, as I started to find partners who could fill in the gaps in my own business. That was a watershed moment for me."

ACTION TWO – HABITS & TIME MANAGEMENT!

"My greatest habit is that I sit down every morning and turn off interruptions. I have my phone on in airplane mode, so email and calls stop for a few hours. I used to have it automatically scheduled; however, it would turn off in the middle of phone calls. Not good when you're in the middle of talking to clients. I had that happen once too many times, so I do it manually now.

I turn on airplane mode, so I don't get calls. I can turn off the internet by turning off the Wi-Fi.

Another program I have that I like is the Dark Room app. It's a desktop app. It blocks out the rest of my computer from distractions.

In the mornings I'm very regimented. I probably get 1,000 to 1,500 words written. That's my greatest habit — that every morning I wake up and write."

ACTION THREE-BE MOTIVATED!

My main motivations are:

"First, would be my wife. I give her props, because if I don't I'll be in trouble. She's also my inspiration. The love of my life, apple of my eye, pain in my ass. The jeweler would not engrave the last part on her wedding ring.

My parents are an inspiration. Both of them owned their own businesses at different times. I come from a very entrepreneurial family. My dad currently owns his own business. My mom owned her own business. My uncle and cousins own their own businesses. My grandfather owned his own business. It wasn't something that was completely foreign to me.

Sometimes my dad and I will talk, and I'll ask him different questions. He's an inspiration, and it keeps me motivated because I know that I'm not alone in what I'm facing. That's one of the biggest things. If I have a question, he usually has an answer. I might not like the answer but he always has an answer.

And my mom does too. She's been very entrepreneurial. She was in sales and owned her own business for 10 or 15 years. We talk about a lot of the creative processes, since she is an artist."

FINAL THOUGHTS

It would be insane to give final thoughts on an interview about myself. It was an April Fools joke that everyone liked, so I kept it in this book. Let's get on with the other stories.

➡️Here's The Story: Josh Alexander

BIO
I have done website consulting for companies all the way from Fortune 100 down to start up organizations. I specialize in profit companies and have other networks for those interested in non-profit organizations. My website is JoshuaAlexander.Net.

My greatest accomplishment I guess is being born with the right problems in the wrong time period.

Josh Alexander

THE DREAM
"Complete accident. I started out as a business-consulting firm, and my first clients asked me who built my website. I told them I did. They asked — Can you build ours? I had just gotten laid off from my job and was starting a new business, so I said sure. Then they sent me referrals, and those people sent me referrals, and it kind of snowballed. That's how I ended up being a website developer.

You hear people complain that you can't make money online. I was lucky enough to have made money from day one."

THE CHALLENGE
"When you start up a business it's always a challenge. The technology, the learning curves and things like that — like I said, I wasn't a web developer at the time — so we had to pick up things and learn as we went along. That's obviously not how you want to do things in business, but that's how it went for us.

I think that's the biggest challenge as you're starting out. You're trying to figure out how everything works in the real world. We started getting requests for different things and we had to figure out what those were so we did a lot of learning as we were growing. We kind of picked up what people wanted and went with that service.

I have the ability to learn fairly quickly, so that helped us immensely. That's the biggest benefit that I've had."

THE ACTIONS
Josh's recipe for success

ACTION ONE-SYSTEMATIZE YOUR BUSINESS

"Recently we've been changing a lot of systems and doing things a lot differently. We've been implementing technologies to help us grow faster. We're definitely getting more business. We've very busy compared to what we used to be.

We have six employees now and a year ago, we had one. It's a huge difference.

It's a huge jump, but at the same time it's been very good for us, and a sign of things to come. We're getting bigger and bigger projects. When we started, we were all doing the small mom and pop shops. Now we're getting more larger scale clients which is good as well.

We're starting to target the things that we should target.

We've learned from our mistakes. When you're small and starting out you make a lot of mistakes, so you learn that you have to change things as you go. That's what we figured out over the years, and we definitely made our share of mistakes like everyone else. No one starts without making mistakes. I think those mistakes teach you the lessons you need to know."

ACTION TWO-PAID TO PLAY ONLINE

"I just like learning this stuff. I enjoy what I do, and I do not know why people complain about this business so much. It's a fun business. We are paid to play online all day. Most companies fire people for what we do on a daily basis, so I cannot see why people have a problem with this industry.

That's pretty much what we do. We play in WordPress all day. WordPress has been the biggest thing that we take care of. I just got my acceptance letter to speak at WordCamp Chicago again so that's three years in a row over there now. I will be talking about plugins and dashboards for new users there. I will probably speak in Milwaukee as well. It's another year of more WordCamps, more speaking engagements, and trying to get out there and do more things.

ACTION THREE-BE ACTIVE IN THE COMMUNITY

We're starting to get some business from that community as well. A lot of overflow development from other development companies. We get business from other tech companies and marketing agencies.

I think our big difference is we looked at the market differently than other companies. Most companies look at how do we target this company, and provide a marketing service to them.

Because I'm not great with people I decided, look, I'm a tech person. We're not the most social people. Let me target other companies that don't do what we do and let them market our stuff for us and we will all share in the profits here. And that's where we've had our advantage. We have 30 or 40 companies around the world sharing our services so I really don't have to do any marketing. The business comes in on a daily business now.

The coding world is changing. We're constantly learning new languages. WordPress is integrating new languages in there. We're starting to see new databases built in for WordPress. You can now use Mango DB in WordPress as opposed to PHP My Admin.

So there are some new things out there that most people even on the development side don't know are out there.

I think marketers in internet marketing are kind of left behind with the technical advantage. They really don't know what's actually available because they don't really study it that much.

It's a huge disconnect between the marketing community and the development community so being on both sides of that community has been a bit of a benefit for us. We can take advantage of the lack of understanding in the marketing community and vice versa. We can take advantage of the lack of marketing concepts in the development community.

We're definitely moving more in the automation fields. Custom automation for marketing for companies. We're looking at augmented reality concepts and programming for that. We're looking at many different angles and at things that will be coming out in the future that will be more prominent instead of just the stuff that's out there right now.

I think one of the problems in the business that everyone does is they look at what do we have today, instead of what's coming out tomorrow. And if we target what's coming out tomorrow we'll have less competition to deal with."

FINAL THOUGHTS

Over the past 3 years, I have been able to see as Josh developed his business systems. One of the sharpest web developers I have ever met. He understands where business and web development meet. Moreover, his inexhaustible energy to be on Skype 24 hours a day, 7 days a week connecting with prospects probably puts me to shame.

➡Here's The Story: Dwan Twyford

BIO

Real estate investor, since 1991. I bought my first dump and went to town! I did all the work on the property myself: paint, tile, and plumbing. After the repairs were completed, I put the house on the market, sold it four days later, made over $20,000 on my first transaction, and never looked back.

One of the reasons new investors fail is they get on a new program. They go to a workshop and buy a home study course, they're all excited at the beginning, but 3 weeks later they're back to watching Cops.

Dwan Bent Twyford

THE DREAM

"I never thought about being a real estate investor. In my 20's I waited tables. It was the 80's, so I was into that whole disco dancing, Studio 34, etc. For work, I mostly just waited tables, tended bar, or something like that.

In my late 20's I got married, decided I definitely wanted to have some kids. I wanted to be a stay at home mom and raise babies. So I'm married, 30 years old, and had my daughter. I thought this is going to be great. I'm going to stay home, I'm going to have kids, and this is going to be fantastic.

When my daughter was 8 months old, my husband and I suddenly parted ways. I'm 30 years old, and have an eight-month-old child. I have no formal education and no real job skills. I thought, 'oh my God, what on earth am I going to do?'

The main thing for me was that I made the decision that I was not going to raise my daughter in the day care system. I thought, I waited all the way until I was 30 to have kids, I thought I picked a good guy, I was crazy about him at the time, and I thought I don't want to put my daughter in day care and go back to work.

What happened was I started searching for something that I could do from my house, and raise my daughter. You have to remember this is 24 years ago. My daughter is 25 now.

Back in those days when you went job hunting you looked in the classified section of the newspaper. There were no jobs on the internet. It was all calling places, setting up job interviews. I was looking around, looking around and couldn't find anything that I'd enjoy doing, and could also do from home.

I was stuck. I didn't want to go back to waiting tables, I didn't want to put her in day care, and I was living on credit cards getting broker by the day. I thought I'm going to keep looking.

I happened to meet a couple of guys that were real estate investors. They would buy houses; they would fix them up and sell them. I remember thinking in my mind — I love to decorate.

Decorating and real estate investing — how hard could it be to do that? That was my thought process. I can decorate, and I can fix things up. How hard can it be? That was my true mindset. When I look back right now, I wonder what I was thinking to start rehabbing with zero skills.

I went the old-fashioned way. I went up to the courthouse in West Palm Beach, Florida. I'd handwrite all of the foreclosure listings for the week, I would go out, and I would go door knocking with this baby hanging on my hip."

THE CHALLENGE

"For me when I got started there were no REA groups, so I didn't have anyone else to talk to about what I was doing. I never knew if I was doing something the right way or not. I knew how to decorate, learned how to rehab, and learned how to do things. Everything really fell together by accident for me.

The hardest thing about getting started was not having anyone train me, teach me, keep me accountable, or encourage me that I was doing things the right way. I mean I didn't know. I would do stuff and I close deals and think — Gosh; I hope this is a good deal.

They didn't have many services for providing comps back then. You really had to learn all the neighborhoods, what the values were, and hope that you were right. My biggest obstacle was just not having anyone to show me how to do it.

When you look back at rehabbing and becoming a real estate investor, it really is a huge business, there's huge money, and it's making millions a month. And it's a huge business to start off completely on your own."

THE ACTIONS

Dwan's recipe for success

ACTION ONE-KEEP TRYING UNTIL YOU SUCCEED!

"I'm going out door knocking. Of course, I didn't have any scripts back then. I didn't have a coach. I just said this is what we do, and here's how we do it. I'm thinking it can't be that hard to do. I'm really winging it.

Everybody is telling me no, no, no. For weeks I got nothing but no's from everybody. I thought God doesn't want me to be a real estate investor, I'm going to have to start looking for something else.

However, I thought I've got this list of people, and I've already mapped them out. We had to map them out using those map books. A little old fashioned. I used that until GPS came out.

I thought I'll just finish off the list that I have, and hopefully somebody will say yes. If not I'll just take it that this isn't what I'm supposed to do, and look for something else.

I'm getting down to the wire and I'm getting really nervous. Everybody is saying no, and nothing is happening.

Then this woman Barbara said, 'I'd love to work with you.' Now I don't know what to do, because nobody ever said yes. She says sure, come on in, and bring your daughter in. I'll work with you. That was it. She said yes, and I went inside her house, we were talking.

I tell her I buy houses, fix them up, and sell them. I'm a rehabber. I don't know what I'm doing. I only had lunch with these guys like twice. She goes okay. We made a deal that I was going to move into her house, make the payments on it, get it rehabbed and she was going to move out.

When we were done, I did a profit split with her on the deal. She moved out and I moved in, because I could not afford to live there, and rent an apartment. I'm living on credit cards. I had no money.

I move into this house. I clean it, put in new carpet, put up some new blinds, and paint the walls. I remember looking around and thinking this place looks terrible.

The kitchen is avocado, old, and outdated and the bathroom is outdated as well. I realized this is what they mean by rehabbing. Painting and putting in carpet and blinds isn't rehabbing. I have all of this stuff that needs to be done, and I don't know how to do anything. I literally started going to Home Depot and taking the Home Depot classes they offer.

I remember taking a class on how to lay tile. I wrote down all the stuff, I gave the guy measurements for my kitchen, they stacked up my trunk with all of these supplies, and I went back and tiled my kitchen floor. I thought you know that wasn't so bad. Then I went back and tiled the bathroom.

I rehabbed this house mostly by myself. At night, my daughter would be sleeping, and I would be building cabinets. I made the screens, washed the pool, painted the house, and did all the things you have to do to rehab it. When my house was done it looked really good. I put it on the market, and sold it for a $22,000 profit."

ACTION TWO-LEARN THE SKILLS YOU NEED TO SUCCEED

"I started literally with zero rehabbing skills. As I said, I thought decorating and rehabbing were the same thing, which you know they clearly are not.

I stayed in rehabbing for 3 or 4 years. In the beginning, I enjoyed doing the physical labor, and I was going through a nasty divorce. What I found out is that rehabbing and tearing down cabinets and tearing things down is good therapy."

ACTION THREE-BE A LEADER

After a few years, she got involved in the Florida real estate investment groups.

"I started a local rehab group down in south Florida. I was teaching on the weekends. I'd have my members come, and I'd do this small workshop. Someone told the Orlando group and then another group and then another group. Before you knew it I was asked to speak all over the United States."

FINAL THOUGHTS

Dwan's story reminds me of the old rags to riches tales you would read in Horatio Alger. However, the truth is that she succeeded, not because of luck or some inherent skill. It was due to her determination and hard work. She outhustled everyone in the room, until she was the center of attention at real estate investor meetings.

➡Here's The Story: Dino Dogan

BIO

I'm the Founder and CEO of Triberr, a truly unique influencer marketing platform. Brands create a campaign page a la Kickstarter and recruit influencers into month long campaigns.

Triberr was born on March 10 2011, and in the first 2 years our focus has been on building the supply side of the influencer equation. We provide unique set of tools influencers can use to amplify their content distribution by tapping into each other's audience.

We have close to 100,000 tribes (groups of bloggers) across 37 categories, each tribe has as few as 15 members to 150 plus.

Most of Forbes' top 50 Social Media influencers are on Triberr. We have a similar penetration pattern across all 37 categories; from tech, to photography, to fashion, and across food, travel, and especially the coveted mom-influencer category.

Frankly, I'm afraid to feel successful because when you feel successful you feel contented and when you feel contented you tend to get lazy and when you get lazy, you get stupid, you start doing silly stuff. It is better that I do not feel successful.

Dino Dogan

THE DREAM

"I had a tribe. Back in 2009, 2010 I had a tribe of bloggers. You know just a group of us. We were reading each other's content, commenting on each other's content, and sharing each other's content. That was infinitely more effective at getting targeted traffic back to my blog than SEO. That's coming from a guy that made a living doing SEO for a brief time.

SEO is good at getting a certain kind of traffic. Transactional traffic where you are not looking to build a relationship. You're just looking to do a transaction, sell a widget or something like that.

But if you're trying to build a community, present yourself as an authority in a specific niche, or building trust amongst people you need a certain targeted type of traffic. My tribe was affording me that traffic. There were about 15 of us, and we couldn't scale out. Imagine going to 15 blogs every day and commenting, and sharing them and scheduling them. It was just so painful.

I thought if this is so effective with 15 people, how effective this would be with 50 or 150 people. The problem is you can't scale it.

So I was like there's got to be a platform out there that allows me to get all of this content in one spot and share it and comment and schedule it from that one spot to get shared to Twitter and Facebook and LinkedIn and so on. It would enable my tribe mates to do the same for me. I spent 3 days looking for a platform like that, couldn't find it, and I was like let's build it. And Dan was in."

THE CHALLENGE

"I had this idea for Triberr, but I couldn't code my way out of a paper bag. So that was challenge #1. It was like, how could I do this?

But I had done some podcasts with Dan back in 2010 on SEO stuff. He's an SEO guy. I fancied myself an SEO guy. We did some podcasts together. I'd essentially yell at him about SEO stuff and Google patents and stuff like that.

I'm not a believer in SEO. SEO is an old game. You can't bet on Google. Google is not in your corner. Google is not sending you traffic. Google is not your friend. I've known this for a long time.

The first challenge was getting someone that could code this. I knew Dan. We started Triberr in 2011. Back then, he had a platform called Flutters, which was way ahead of the game. I think he started in like 2009 and he still had it in 2011. He was essentially Vine without a six-second time limit. That's all it was. His platform Flutters was Twitter for video is essentially, what Vine and Instagram are.

I knew he had coding chops. We had this relationship, and I had this idea. I contacted him on a Thursday, we got together on a Wednesday, Monday night we had a prototype, and 3 weeks later, we were inviting beta users.

We're always in beta and we're still not where we want to be. That's one of the greatest challenges. When you're building your own platform, one of the greatest challenges is having this big vision and not getting there yesterday. It's like you can't get there now. You have to take it one little, tiny, painful step at a time."

THE ACTIONS

Dino's recipe for success

ACTION ONE – MONEY IS GOOD!

"We monetized Triberr 3 weeks into its existence. That's first of all. We had virtual currency called bones. We don't have that anymore. We had our first sale on week 4, one month into the platform existing and I think it was for $10.

We were ecstatic. I remember where I was. I was in Tucson, AZ. I was chilling by the pool. I was doing some stuff on my computer and I saw a transaction come through PayPal in my e-mail. I reached out for my phone. I'm about to dial Dan and Dan's calling me, because he saw the transaction. He's going nuts over it in New York. So that was really cool."

ACTION TWO – TRUST YOUR BLOG

To this day, Dino knows that his greatest weapon in spreading the word about Triberr is through his blog.

"That's how I built Triberr. The only reason Triberr exists is because I had a blog, and I had a few hundred people who were paying attention to me on that blog."

ACTION THREE – TELL YOUR TRIBE ABOUT YOUR PRODUCT

"When we built Triberr, I said to those people — Go signup for Triberr. They were like Triberr. What's Triberr? I said don't worry about it. Just go signup. We need beta testers and they did. And those people were the initial user base on Triberr.

Today we have a zero marketing budget. We like it that way. All the promotion that we do starts with our blog. It's how we communicate to our users. It's how I communicate to my audience. If you don't have a blog, you don't have a voice so get a blog."

FINAL THOUGHTS

Dino's words about how he still feels that he is not successful really hit home. He was not the first person to tell me this, but I thought his explanation was one of the best. He really believes that he is "behind in accomplishing his goals." That is inspiring, because it means he is still hungry to achieve more.

➡Here's The Story: Dik Muller

BIO

Serial entrepreneur successful in delivering alternative income streams through team building that can be passed on to family and children. Providing individuals with income that never ends.

> It's a tough road, don't let anybody kid you. It's very hard work, because there's only about 2% of the people that are entrepreneurial enough and want to work hard enough to make it a success. So it's turning over a lot of rocks.
>
> *Dik Muller*

THE DREAM

"As a young man, I was a very talented artist. I got my first scholarship to the Art Institute at the age of eight. Art has always been my thing.

I graduated from high school, went to art school, realized that was a difficult way to earn a living. I wanted to be a portrait painter. Hello?

I went back to school. Took some classes at Northwestern Kellogg's, then went out, and bought the company that I had worked for as a kid in high school. That began an almost 30-year run of being in the marketing services business."

THE CHALLENGE

"I kind of expect everybody I'm around to have the same kind of feeling about accomplishment I do. I oftentimes will, through a fault of my own, invest in individuals that don't turn out to be what I want. I want everybody to be successful, but you can't drag them kicking and screaming to success because they aren't going to go."

THE ACTIONS

Dik's recipe for success

ACTION ONE-IF YOU WANT IT, GO ALL OUT

"I think the greatest lesson in business is if you decide you want a client. You have to go way out on a limb.

One was with a company called Fidelity Electronics, who developed a game called Chess Challenger. We had their point of sale business, and I wanted the whole business.

This is in the late '70s.

They were going to have a national sales meeting. I said to the owner that I'd like to present my thinking about where you guys should go with your business. He said, "I don't care. Whatever you want to do. Bring it to the sales meeting."

This goes back before the wonderful digital age. We did a slide presentation. We had a bank of 40 slide projectors all synchronized. We had a technical guy who was a wizard. We took this whole 9 yards of stuff to Miami. We went through the whole program. It took about 20 minutes. It was like a movie show.

Their ad agency was in the audience. When we were done the guy came up to me and said, "I guess you deserve to get the business."

You know when you're a winner it didn't cost anything to say — 'you're right.' I know he wasn't happy, but the reality is we went the extra mile.

We did all of their television commercials. We did their super bowl commercials. It was wonderful. You have to go out there and do it."

ACTION TWO-CREATIVITY

"I'll tell you in a word what you need to be an entrepreneur-Creativity. You've got to really train yourself to say everyday — what I did yesterday, what didn't work? And what can we do today that's creative and different. That's not easy."

ACTION THREE-ACTION BEGETS ACTION

"The way to get motivated for me, you only have one life to live. I do not want to spend my whole life living in a corner of one closet when the world is my house. I need to get out of the closet, and the only way I can do that is to be very successful. The more successful I am, the more of the house I can see.

Success breeds success. The more successful you are the more successful people you meet, the more the world opens."

FINAL THOUGHTS

Dik has an interesting career. He is definitely of the breed that believes business is all about relationships. That is what makes him such a powerful business leader. He connects with people, and focuses on creative ways to make their business better.

➡Putting it All Together

What direction should you take with your business? How can you go from dreams to success yourself? My desire is that after reading the stories of the Gappers who went from dreams to success, your mind is full of prospects for your own business.

You need to find your direction, and a way to let that direction be a beacon of hope to others.

To do that, you need to know not only why you might want to take the figurative door number one, but also why that is a better option. Stories help us understand. My hope is that the stories we discussed in this book not only brought you to laughter or tears, but also made you consider your own progress in business.

Being able to judge the changes you have made to start your business is truly a feat. So many quit after what seems to be an endless loop of expectations and failure.

Personally, I remember after my first paid webinar series was whether this was the best it was going to get. I struggled for over a month to bring prospects into the class only to make $333 on a four week webinar series.

"That was it," I thought. "Should I quit now?"

Looking back, I see that this was one step among many on the path to success. Every time I felt myself dragging and getting stuck in that continuous loop, something amazing would happen. You have to believe. The loop is something we all must in the gap between dreams and success.

Understand that what you do in the gap is important. When you carry that dream with you long enough, trudging it on your back through every challenge that comes your way you will eventually reach your goal.

MIND THE NEXT GAP

As I reflect upon the interviews and research over the past year creating this book, I think about another sobering and exciting fact: the gap never ends.

Yes, there is a point when you can quantify success. That point, where what you are doing is a little easier. It is also then, you will look to expand and begin anew.

As entrepreneurs we create massive success, only to realize that it is not enough. We go in an endless series of gaps. Each project, each business is a new gap.

Look at the great business owners today, who build an empire by evening, only to start on their next one in the morning.

Those who follow one path long enough to reach success will tell you that it only happened, because of the first gap. Without that, nothing else was possible.

In the DNA of every great entrepreneur lies a fiery passion yearning to set forth on this world a better vision for the future.

It all begins with that first step, the first dream. In taking you down the path between dreams and success, I hope we provided you with a guide that will eliminate a few failures, and give you some of the "aha" moments you need to create your own success.

My hope in writing *Start Up Gap* is you found the stories in this book, worthy of your memory, so when you face them in your own business you confidently steer your business in the right direction.

That you too may go from dreams to success!

➡Bonus

Now that you have the ideas, you need the tools to execute everything properly?

What online resources do you need to get your business running smoothly?

Stop guessing, and start knowing with our free add-on to 30 Minute Businesses, *101 Online Tools: What You Need To Succeed.*

In this no-nonsense eBook, you will get simple, easy to use tools that can make you more effective in every aspect of your business.

http://startupgap.com/101-free-online-tools/

➡️If You Liked *Start Up Gap,* Check Out My Other Books

 **Learning from Failure** is a joint effort of 11 entrepreneurs who have experienced failure in their business and life, and bounced back. Failure is a lesson on the road to success.

Get your copy at *http://startupgap.com/learningfromfailure*

 **30 Minute Businesses** shows you 30 different business ideas you can use to start up a business. This eBook will provide the answers along with the initial action steps to help you get started in the field that has the most opportunity for you.

Get your copy at *http://startupgap.com/30minutebusiness*

 For those who want to really build a long-lasting business based on relationships then this introduction to online marketing book, **E Marketing Experiences** is for you.

Get your copy at *http://andynathan.net/amazon*

➡Special Thanks!

I want to give a special thanks to all the people who made this book possible. To all the Gappers who gave of their time for the interview. Joanna Chlasta and Candace Chira, thank you, thank you, thank you for your amazing work on this project.

Thank you Bernard Small, Josh Alexander, and Sotiris Bassakaropolis for your valuable insights.

Need to thank my mom and dad for their insights into the book. Also, my mom designed the cover and many of the graphics in the book. This would be an ugly book without her help.

Furthermore, thanks to my little sister Kim for your support.

Finally, thanks to my wife who had the patience to deal with my rants and ravings when I had writers block, and gave me her honest opinion of what she liked and did not like of the book.

➡Let's Connect

As someone who is an avid social media user and blogger, I am always looking to connect with people online. Here are some of my social media profiles. Feel free to reach out to me. Let me know what you thought of the book (I have a delicate ego, so be kind).

Facebook
http://www.facebook.com/andynathan

LinkedIn
http://www.linkedin.com/in/andrewmarcnathan

Google+
http://plus.google.com/+AndyNathan

Twitter
http://www.twitter.com/andynathan
http://www.twitter.com/TheStartUpGap

Blogs
http://startupgap.com
http://andynathan.net